A CONSCIOUS LEADERSHIP COLLECTIVE

BRAVE SPACES BOLD CONVERSATIONS

FREE YOUR MIND, THE REST WILL FOLLOW

AN ANTHOLOGY PRESENTED BY:

CHANTÉE L. CHRISTIAN

FOREWORD BY: REGGIE HUBBARD

A CONSCIOUS LEADERSHIP COLLECTIVE

BRAVE SPACES BOLD CONVERSATIONS

FREE YOUR MIND, THE REST WILL FOLLOW

AN ANTHOLOGY PRESENTED BY:

CHANTÉE L. CHRISTIAN

FOREWORD BY: REGGIE HUBBARD

CONSCIOUS AUTHORS

B. MARIE ADAMS | ERNEST BONASERA | BRIANA BROWN, M.ED

WHITNEY CARRINGTON | BRANDON T. JONES | SUMMER C. MARTIN

NAYSHONDRA MERCER, MA, CPC, ELI-MP | SEEMA M. PATEL

M.C. TYLER | ANGELA DIXON WILLIAMS

Published in the United States by: CC Media, LLC (a subsidiary of My Best SHIFT, LLC)
www.ccmediaproductions.net, www.mybestshift.com,
Arlington, Virginia 22206

Cover design by MaeArt Creative
Cover photography by Life of a Fat Kid, LLC
Interior design by CC Media, LLC and MaeArt Creative

CC Media, LLC books may be purchased in bulk for businesses, educational, or promotional use. For information, contact info@mybestshift.com.

Paperback ISBN: 979-8-9995433-9-4

First Edition: April 2026

ALSO BY CC MEDIA, LLC

(a subsidiary of My Best SHIFT, LLC)

A Conscious Leadership Collective: Volume I: Leading From Within

Awareness Put Me On: Leading By Choice, Thriving By Design

12 Shades of Empowerment: Monthly Affirmations for Black Women

(Coloring Book)

You're Dope AF (52 Affirmations)

You could be anywhere in the world, yet you chose to be here, with us. For that, we are deeply grateful.

This book is for anyone who has ever felt unseen, unheard, misunderstood, or like their voice did not matter. For those who have questioned whether speaking up would change anything, or if anyone was truly willing to listen.

May these pages remind you that your voice carries power. Your lived experience holds wisdom. And the conversations we avoid often hold the very breakthroughs we need.

"Brave Spaces, Bold Conversations" is a radical act of choosing truth over silence, curiosity over defensiveness, and connection over comfort. It is for those willing to stay present long enough to understand, brave enough to speak honestly, and humble enough to listen deeply.

We see you. Keep speaking.

We hear you. Keep listening.

We are in this together.

We got this!

TABLE OF **CONTENTS**

SETTING THE STAGE

PART I
THE TRUTH BENEATH THE SILENCE

"If I didn't define myself for myself, I would be crunched into other people's fantasies for me and eaten alive." —Audre Lorde

PART II
THE COST OF STAYING QUIET

"Our lives begin to end the day we become silent about things that matter." —Dr. Martin Luther King Jr.

PART III
CHOOSING THE HARD CONVERSATION

"Courage starts with showing up and letting ourselves be seen." — Brené Brown

PART IV
LEADING WITHOUT ARMOR

"The work of the leader is to create conditions where the truth can be told." —Parker J. Palmer

EXTENDING THE SHIFT

SETTING THE STAGE

ENTERING BRAVE SPACES

A collective invitation into truth, tension, and transformation

"When you talk, you are only repeating what you already know. But if you listen, you may learn something new"

—Dalai Lama

FOREWORD

BY REGGIE HUBBARD

INTEGRITY OVER PERFORMANCE

From my personal experiences as an activist, movement leader, yoga/meditation teacher, visionary disruptor, and most recently a stroke survivor, I have learned the wisdom and necessity of turning toward the shadowy things we would rather not deal with to bring about the changes necessary for healing and transformation. In fact, the only way through tough times is just that—through them. By courageously confronting what you'd rather avoid—with an open heart, curious mind and a sense of what's possible rather than fear of what isn't possible—miraculous things can emerge.

Let me explain….

On April 1st, 2024, I had a right parietal lobe stroke, impacting my left leg and eliminating motor neurological function in my left foot. At a moment's notice, I went from carefree human being en route to a friend's wedding to fighting for my life, hundreds of miles away from home and deeply unsure about what the future held. I was partially paralyzed, with concurrent diagnoses of hypertension, diabetes and the lingering complications from the stroke—something that surely wasn't on my 2024 vision board.

Of course, I had the battery of normal psychological responses. How did this happen? What did I do wrong? How could the yoga and wellness dude succumb to a stroke? Will I ever recover from this? I quickly had to have many sobering conversations with myself and medical professionals as I attempted to pick up the pieces from my rapid descent to rock bottom as far as my health was concerned. All of the things I would get to later or been ignoring (consciously or subconsciously), I had to deal with then and there. There was no way to healing without dealing with my feelings.

To rise from the ashes of this experience, I had to honestly and compassionately confront years of neglected family history, suspect eating habits and avoidance of medical checkups because "I don't trust doctors." I vulnerably shared my journey with everyone—asking for help, telling people not to play the games I had been playing with avoiding the doctor and not checking my blood pressure, sharing my journey of learning how to walk again. It was impossible for me to avoid the hard things anymore. And by turning toward what I once ignored with courage and grace—literally putting one foot in front of the other—the seeds for my renaissance were planted and made manifest.

My personal experience with stroke and recovery offers an ideal vantage point from which to view the microcosm of what we are dealing with writ large. As a collective, we are living in times where longheld secrets and inconvenient truths are being laid bare for all to see. For years we have deluded ourselves into thinking that if we look the other way, things will sort themselves out—or at a bare minimum, someone else will take care of them. Keeping the peace is rooted in conflict avoidance. We would rather have cute conversations than confront hard truths. A ruthless pursuit of efficiency has rendered methodical, patient and purposeful progress a waste of time.

And how has this delusion, conditioned avoidance and reliance on ineffective communication served us? Our most seemingly intractable social, societal and spiritual problems look as impossible to confront as ever, let alone consider any solutions. Diatribes, division and dehumanization are now romanticized as desirable rather than the hard work of honest conversation, connection and compassion. What are we supposed to do in such an environment?

Allow me to offer a few thoughts….

It is incumbent upon those of us who hope for something better to speak out against current norms that have not served us for a while and definitely are not able (nor designed) to meet the moment at hand. You cannot build something new by clinging to something old.

We must individually and collectively lean into what we have thus far avoided: difficult conversations, emotional presence, candor and truth. When we begin to do this, we realize:

- The things we have been taught to fear have been the way forward the entire time.
- We have more in common than we have been conditioned to believe.
- The solutions we seek are not as distant as we might imagine, and more people are inclined to believe in and work toward them—they just have to be expressed.

This collection of essays makes the case that the way we have been doing things clearly isn't working and the times require the careful cultivation of brave spaces and bold conversations—with ourselves and one another. The authors thoughtfully articulate from lived experience the value in being contrarian to prevailing norms; integrity over performative antics; the notion that rest and taking your time is productive; embracing disruption as a force of innovation, transformation and integration—all prescient, medicinal topics for these turbulent times.

It has often been said, "Fortune favors the brave," almost to the point of it being cliché. But within each cliché lies a kernel of truth. Let us all put on the mantle of bravery, claim the fortune that comes with it and share the spoils of our collective healing and liberation in a world in desperate need of courage, creativity and connection.

ABOUT THE AUTHOR

REGGIE HUBBARD

Reggie Hubbard is the Founder and Chief Serving Officer of Active Peace LLC, a wellness and social impact organization dedicated to cultivating well-being as a foundation for leadership, activism, and collective healing. A nationally recognized teacher, strategist, and sound healer, his work lives at the intersection of wellness, justice, and community transformation.

A stroke survivor and former political strategist, Reggie has worked at the highest levels of U.S. politics and grassroots advocacy, bringing a unique perspective to the integration of personal well-being and civic engagement. His lived experience informs a body of work that challenges individuals and institutions to move beyond performative practices toward embodied awareness, compassion, and sustainable impact.

Through Active Peace, he has developed and led transformative programming in partnership with leading institutions such as the Kripalu Center for Yoga & Health. His work includes pioneering initiatives focused on grief, collective healing, and the well-being of marginalized communities, including Permission and Refuge: Healing Retreat for Men of Color and the How We Heal virtual series.

Reggie's thought leadership has been featured across respected platforms including Essence, Yoga Journal, the Omega Institute, the Mind & Life Institute, Sounds True Foundation, and the Be Here Now Network. He was recently named one of Yoga Journal's Top Yoga Teachers to Watch in 2026.

A global citizen based in the Washington, DC, area, Reggie continues to guide leaders, organizations, and communities toward deeper alignment, healing, and justice-centered leadership.

INTRODUCTION

CHANTÉE L. CHRISTIAN

"Courage is contagious. A critical mass of brave leaders is the foundation of an intentionally courageous culture." — Brené Brown

Have you ever left a conversation and started replaying it, over and over again?

Thinking about what you wish you had said, but didn't. The boundary you should have held but softened. The truth you felt in your spirit, but edited for the sake of comfort, compliance, or not rocking the boat.

If any of that sounds remotely familiar, no worries.

You are in the right place.

Welcome to a collective exploration into the power of (re)defining leadership: *A Conscious Leadership Collective*, Volume II: *Brave Spaces, Bold Conversations.* Volume I: *Leading From Within* was about awareness, alignment, and the courageous work of looking inward—and this volume is about what happens next.

Not the polished voice we use in boardrooms or bios—the honest one we use when we think no one is around. The one that tells the truth when silence would be easier. The one that disrupts comfort to make space for something more real.

Because at some point, awareness demands expression. And expression almost always requires conversation. Not the polite, surface-level kind of conversation that keeps everything neat and tidy. The real kind. The kind where truth shows up, sometimes uninvited, and asks us to deal with it anyway.

Truth be told, leadership does not transform through silence. It transforms through conversations.

Full disclaimer: This book is a curation of real stories from real leaders. Truth-tellers, disruptors, and change agents who are redefining what leadership looks and feels like when it's led from within. It is not designed to be a full-on playbook. It is meant to be a mirror. I am an avid believer that you don't attract what you want; you attract who you are. And through that lens, certain chapters and authors will feel like they're speaking directly to you because in many ways, they are.

FROM AWARENESS TO EXPRESSION

Volume I of this series, *Leading From Within*, invited readers to begin with self-awareness. To look inward. To examine identity, integrity, and authenticity as the foundation of conscious leadership.

Awareness alone is not the final destination. At some point, awareness requires expression. Awareness without action becomes stagnation. And expression almost always requires conversation.

And that is where this book lives. *Brave Spaces, Bold Conversations* explores what happens when leaders stop editing themselves for comfort and start telling the truth. Not recklessly. Not performatively. But with presence, discernment, and courage.

Across these chapters, brave space is not theory. It's lived experience. These authors do not write from the mountaintop of polished leadership, but from the middle of reckoning. From hospital rooms and boardrooms. From classrooms and executive tables. From marriages, restructurings, diagnoses, identity shifts, and moments that demanded courage when comfort would have been easier.

Each story asks a version of the same question: *Who benefits from my silence and/or complicity?*

(RE)INTRODUCTION

Before we get too far into the introduction of this powerful body of work, allow me to (re)introduce myself. I'm Chantée L. Christian, your official *Ambassador of Awareness* on this expedition. The cultural nods sprinkled throughout this collection of books is very intentional. You're welcome! Consider them a gift from me to you.

Some of you may already know me from *Awareness Put Me On* or *Leading From Within*. Others may be meeting me for the first time.

Either way, welcome. I'm excited to be on this journey with you.

Who am I? I'm a catalyst for growth, change, and inspired action. Through my work as a management consultant, executive coach, curator of brave conversations, multiple-time bestselling author and publisher, I've had the honor of helping people uncover their voice, expand their impact, and lead with intention. I've had the privilege of creating spaces where stories challenge norms, shift narratives, and create ripple effects far beyond what any single voice could accomplish alone. Spaces where people feel brave enough to tell their truth.

As the founder of CC Media, LLC, the award-winning multimedia imprint behind the *My Best SHIFT* podcast, the *Unspoken Truths* series, and the international bestsellers *Awareness Put Me On* and *Leading From Within,* I've had the privilege of cultivating stories that move hearts, shift minds, and create rippling effects far beyond my wildest dreams. I expect nothing less from *Brave Spaces, Bold Conversations.*

Together, we are setting the tone for what's next.

Transformation over tradition. Awareness over autopilot. Intention in every step.

THE COURAGE TO SPEAK

As your *Ambassador of Awareness* on this reflective and introspective journey, I invite you to pause and consider:

- Who are you when no one's watching?
- What if you stopped editing yourself for comfort and chose connection over compliance or complacency?
- More importantly, what conscious (or unconscious) place are you speaking and leading from?

Remember, whether it's personal or professional, who you are in one space is who you are in all spaces. It may manifest or look different depending on the environment, but the result is the same.

Buckle up, friend! You are about to embark on a transformative adventure, one that begins with that opening question.

As you dive into the pages of *Brave Spaces, Bold Conversations*, I invite you to not just think about them intellectually. Sit with them from a space of deep introspection rooted in bravery and alive with a wild courageous energy that stirs something up in your soul. This isn't just about reflection. It is about reclamation—of self, of truth, of the power you've always held.

One of the most fascinating things about human behavior is that we often know the truth long before we are willing to say it.

We clearly see the dysfunction in a process or system. We feel the misalignment in a relationship. We recognize when something no longer works, long before others do. And yet, we hesitate and second-guess ourselves. We edit ourselves. We soften the message for the sake of peace and harmony.

Sometimes we even gaslight ourselves. And other times, we allow others to gaslight us into believing that keeping quiet is the most responsible choice for the collective.

Somewhere along the way we learned that keeping the peace meant avoiding conflict, that professionalism meant emotional distance. That leadership meant having the answers instead of asking the "hard" questions.

The authors in this book challenge that dated narrative.

This anthology is a space for truth-telling. A space where authenticity is not a buzzword but a practice. A place to honor the messy, magical process of becoming. Curated by a diverse collective of leaders, each consciously redefining what it means to lead in today's world.

These pages hold lived experiences. Stories shaped by moments of disruption, reckoning, and choice. Moments where avoidance was no longer an option and honesty (with self and others) became the only path forward.

Because leadership is more than performance. It's presence. It's alignment. It's the willingness to be seen without armor. AND this redefined or reimagined version of leadership is an open invitation for you to return to who you've always been—before the titles, before the expectations, before the noise and the world tried to convince you otherwise.

We have intentionally cultivated a space where leaders feel brave enough to go beyond the surface—the same surface-level narratives that have cluttered bookshelves for far too long (no shade... *Okay,* maybe just a little).

These authors dug deep so *you* could feel seen, heard, inspired, and reminded that you are not alone. Brené Brown reminds us, "You can't get to courage without rumbling with vulnerability." Let me assure you, the courage shown in these pages is undeniable. Naval Ravikant once said, "To write a great book, you must first become the book."

These chapters embody those statements.

They share moments where silence stopped being protection and started becoming a limitation. Moments where truth disrupted comfort and made space for growth. The common thread among these authors is that they chose courage. It was rarely perfect. Almost never comfortable. And yet wildly intentional.

And through those moments of conscious choice, something powerful emerged: clarity, accountability, connection, and the possibility for something new. Because bold conversations rarely begin with volume. They begin with courage to stand ten toes down and say it with your chest.

IMAGINATION, DESIRE, AND CHOICE

Our imagination shapes our reality. Neville Goddard once said that imagination is the greatest force in human existence because it allows us to envision what does not yet exist.

Leadership works the same way. Before systems change, someone must imagine something different. Before conversations shift reality, someone must believe a different outcome is possible.

Desire is often the beginning of that process. It is not wishful thinking. It is awareness. It is the recognition that something different exists and of the willingness to move toward it.

When we become aware of what we want to create, we begin to see the conversations that must happen to make it real. Conversations are usually the right next step a.k.a. inspired action.

To be very clear, those conversations require a lot of courage. The type of courage that challenges assumptions. The type of courage that is willing to disrupt outdated narratives. The courage to imagine something different and speak it into existence.

These authors didn't just write about brave spaces and bold conversations theoretically; they *lived* them. Sure, you might find a few soundbites or steps to help you curate bold spaces and have brave conversations. But what you will really find is emotional resonance, space for reflection, and raw, unfiltered truth.

Their stories reveal the pivotal moments when silence was no longer an option. When saying the thing that needed to be said became the only path forward. When courage showed up not as perfection, but as presence.

And in those moments, their truth created movement. Their honesty created possibility. And their conversations became the catalyst for change. Because sometimes the most courageous thing to do is to say the thing that everyone else is thinking but no one has been brave enough to say.

YOUR INVITATION TO GO WITHIN

I invite you to be an active participant in your transformation. This isn't passive reading. This is work: personal, professional, soul, spiritual work a.k.a. leadership development. Here's your assignment, should you choose to accept it:

1. **Engage Authentically**: Show up with curiosity and an open heart. These stories are meant to be felt, not just read.
2. **Exercise Your Discomfort Muscle**: Let go of the need to agree with everything. This isn't an echo chamber for what you already believe. Stretch. Reflect. Be willing to see things differently.
3. **Personalize Your Experience**: Highlight, annotate, journal, or use whatever tools help you capture what resonates. What stings. What stays with you.

4. **Redefine Leadership**: Explore how to bring more presence, more truth, and more alignment into the spaces where you lead and live. Ask yourself, *What does it look like to lead with brave spaces and bold conversations within?*

Brave spaces are not environments someone else creates for us. They are environments we choose to cultivate with others. This isn't a script. It's an invitation. A conversation. A co-created space for brave reflection, honest dialogue, and the big SHIFT. *Brave Spaces, Bold Conversations* is your mirror, your map, and maybe your moment of reckoning.

Think of this as your leadership Vegas—what happens here, stays here, until you are ready to share. Because if these pages do what they are meant to do, you will find yourself asking different questions, having different conversations, and showing up with a different level of courage than before.

And when you do, do it from a place of alignment and conscious choice. Let this be your brave space. Your safe space. A sacred ecosystem for growth, awareness, acceptance, authenticity, and transformation.

The real power of *Brave Spaces, Bold Conversations* is not what happens inside these pages. It's in what you do with what meets you here.

Let's get into it!

PART I

THE TRUTH BENEATH THE SILENCE

Identity, Belonging, and the Stories That Shape Our Leadership

"If I didn't define myself for myself, I would be crunched into other people's fantasies for me and eaten alive."

—Audre Lorde

CHAPTER ONE

SEEMA M. PATEL

WHEN COMFORT COSTS EVERYTHING

"Owning our story can be hard but not nearly as difficult as spending our lives running from it." —Brené Brown

Connection has always come easily to me. Belonging has not. I learned early how to read a room, adapt quickly, and become who I needed to be to fit in. Over time, that ability became my superpower. It is how I built relationships with my family, my children, my colleagues, and even people I had just met. It is how I earned trust, created safety, and found my place in the world.

Family is supposed to be where connection runs deepest, a place where we can be our authentic selves without judgment. But that has not always been my reality. Some of the hardest connections I have had to navigate have been within my own family. It is where I believed I could be the most vulnerable yet often felt the least safe to be. So, I learned to hide behind a façade of smiles and comfort, believing I was doing the right thing. The *appropriate* thing.

What I did not understand then was the cost. Connection often required editing myself for comfort. Keeping the peace meant keeping parts of me hidden. Especially at home, where I wanted to be most seen and felt the least able to be fully myself.

That tension has shaped much of my life and leadership style, and it leaves me with this question: What happens when we stop editing ourselves for comfort and choose connection over compliance or complacency?

YOU DON'T BELONG

Growing up, I never felt like I belonged anywhere. We moved around often, so I was constantly learning to connect with others, create new friendships, and build trust quickly. The toughest move was from Canada to the States as a young teenager. I had to leave a diverse, open-minded community for a very white, conservative small town in the Midwest.

After being the shiny new penny and getting a lot of attention from my classmates, I learned all too quickly that the friendliness I received from my classmates and teachers around me was surface-level and fake.

In seventh grade, I began to feel that this was not the place I could ever feel at home. Connection at a deeper level was now beyond my grasp. Comfort, complacency, and yet another façade became how folks survived each other, and I learned to do the same so I could survive until I was old enough to reassert myself and fulfill my needs for connection and belonging.

My immediate family, my parents and my baby sister, became my refuge for vulnerability and connection, where I could let down my walls. Well... to a point at least.

As an only child for the first six years, I was quiet, listened, obeyed, and followed my parents' rules. You did not question; you just did as you were told. You did not verbalize your thoughts. In my South Asian culture, this showed respect to your elders within the immediate and extended family. Seeing approval in my elders' eyes always made me feel proud, knowing I did something right. My parents were kind, loving, social people who taught me to be the same, but to keep order, you followed the rules. I thought that was how a child was supposed to be. It made me feel good about myself.

This set in motion a deep, lifelong desire to be liked and valued. To know that I belong and that I matter.

WHAT JUST HAPPENED?

All my life, I was going to be a doctor, or so I thought. From age six, I was being groomed to accomplish this. Everything worked toward this path: volunteering at hospitals, straight A's, honor roll, endless test prep. I never questioned it. This was the South Asian aspiration, a doctor or engineer. The measurement of success through financial freedom and the social status that came with it.

Then came a self-realization during the summer between my junior and senior year of college: I was not following the path I genuinely believed in. I did not want to be a doctor. Even though I would be financially set for life, I did not want the life of a doctor, especially a female doctor. I questioned this with my dad, considering engineering instead. He was an engineer; most of our friends were doctors. He told me that engineering was not the right choice, that it would not provide financial freedom. I understand now that he felt inferior to those around him because he could not provide the big house and materialistic things he saw that others possessed. He did not want me to experience those feelings. So, I continued on the medical path until I could not anymore. The stress on my body and mind meant that I had to do something I rarely do, to take a chance and do something different.

COMPLIANCE BECOMES CATASTROPHIC

I knew I had to tell my parents, who had supported me emotionally and financially through all of this, that I had changed my mind. How was I going to do this? Their eldest daughter, the "good" girl, the one who followed all their rules and guidance, would thoroughly disappoint them.

It was a gut-wrenching decision. They were going to be mad; they were going to hate me, feel that I wasted their time, damaged their pride, and squandered their money. What made it worse was that I did not have an alternative career path determined. No plan B. I just knew I did not want to be a doctor. I wanted my dad to be proud of me, and now I was going to ruin all of that. I was terrified of the disappointment in his eyes, berating myself with self-editing questions: Why can't I just go along with it? Why can't I just appease them?

That weekend, I drove home, rehearsing the words I would never be able to take back. I saw shock, disappointment, and anger. I vividly recall the moment when I broke our close connection. I felt it in the pit of my stomach. I was a daddy's girl, and I could see him withdraw. His shoulders dropped and he couldn't look at me. It hurt my heart. I broke that close bond, and I was never going to get it back.

Then a bigger bomb dropped: my dad announced that since I was not going to medical school, we would start looking at matrimonial sites. This was to be my next path. No longer poised for my own success and abilities, but to be thought of as someone who *needed* to be tied to the success of another.

I sat there, stunned. Matrimonial sites. Arranged marriage. At twenty-one years old, my value had just been recalculated: not a doctor, diminished in value only to be someone's wife. The logic was brutal and clear. I had broken the contract by choosing myself, so now he would choose for me.

"We've been too lenient," he said. "Given you too much freedom."

My mother sat silent. The woman who had been my confidante, whom I thought would protect me, said nothing. That silence broke something deeper than my father's anger. I was not only losing his approval; I was learning that my authenticity had a price no one was willing to pay but me.

Something solidified within me that day. I would comply, but I had stopped believing compliance would ever help me regain what I had lost. I felt frightened, emotionally exhausted, and scared.

This was not about one conversation or one decision. It was about the moment I stopped changing myself to fit my parents' vision. I was not portraying a good, obedient child, and the consequence of my pushback was that my dad felt he needed to regain some control as a parent that he felt he had lost.

This decision changed the course of my life entirely. Financially dependent, young, and starving for his approval, choosing my own path felt nothing like empowerment. Every following decision became a negotiation: Will this be agreeable to my parents? The question of what *I* wanted did not even make the list.

IT IS MESSY AND CONFUSING

From here on out, I was emotionally alone. I was going to have to manage it all on my own. After the initial shock of my announcement and my dad's declaration, we did not have much of a discussion about what was next for me academically. I knew I would finish my pre-med degree and pursue another degree where I could repurpose my gained credits. This was also when I lost complete confidence in myself. It made me feel valueless and clueless. I did not trust myself or my decisions anymore. This negative sense of self and the strained relationship with my ambitions continue to plague me to this day.

I felt like a failure. My friends were celebrating engagement rings and job offers in their chosen fields while I scrambled to salvage a degree from pre-med credits I couldn't waste. The contrast was stark. At group dinners, I'd plaster on my supportive smile and ask about wedding venues and starting salaries, then cry once I got home and was in my bed alone.

My relationship with my parents had splintered so deeply, we spoke in careful half-sentences, never mentioning the weekend that broke us. My friends didn't understand the paralysis I felt. Most nights, I'd lie awake, chest tight with anxiety—no clear path forward, and the looming threat of matrimonial site browsing hanging over me. I didn't know what I wanted, so I couldn't ask for help. What was wrong with me?

I learned to compartmentalize. I stopped searching for answers and started surviving—focusing on day-to-day classes, saying yes to whatever opportunity appeared. Not because it aligned with any vision, but because it was there and it moved me forward or at least gave the appearance of it. This haphazard approach became my pattern for 30 years. I took whichever job seemed viable rather than what I wanted. I was never in the driver's seat of my career. I was always the passenger.

That need for approval bled into every area of my life—work, marriage, friendships, even with my children. I needed everyone to like me, to value me, to confirm I mattered. So, I became agreeable and avoided conflict. The need to assert my true self had backfired. Even though I do not regret refusing to become a doctor, there is a long shadow that has affected every decision since.

Compliance became my survival strategy, my default operating system in all my relationships. In the marriage I stayed in for 23 years, I remember sitting at dinners, watching myself perform. My husband would say something, decide about our money, our kids' schooling, our future plans, and I would feel the "no" rise in my throat. But I would swallow it, smile, nod.

Across the table, I would catch my reflection in the window: a woman agreeing to a life she did not choose, again. I was doing to myself what I had sworn I would never let anyone do to me again. I just did not know how to stop.

I taught my boys that compliance is safety. I modeled this for them. I expected this from them, too. I now realize that I did the same thing to them that my parents did to me, especially when they were young. It was not until they were in high school that I realized my mistakes. I started shifting my teaching by verbalizing the positives and negatives of compliance to them and giving them space to stop self-editing with me.

I was exhausted from constantly self-editing to meet everyone else's expectations and needs. At work, I continued to take on a variety of roles over the years and multiple responsibilities because it was what my leaders believed I was good at. I agreed since it was pitched as a forward movement in my career. I lost my career path by being agreeable and complacent in following what others thought my career path should be. My superpower of connection had become a people-pleasing connection with truth.

My imposter syndrome heightened to higher levels. I believed that I did not know anything and that I was not good enough in any aspect of my life. I allowed these fears to take hold of me and bury themselves deep inside of me. To others, I showed extreme confidence and a "know everything" attitude, but the reality was that I still did not fully believe in myself. Even when I led my own team and received a 98% engagement score by my staff, I still felt as though it was a mistake. I felt I still had so much to improve as a leader. I had become invisible to myself. I struggled with positive feedback. I connected with opportunities for improvement, but if someone told me I did something right, I questioned their authenticity. They were just being nice. We are our worst critics.

REALIZATION AND REINVENTION

I learned a lot through experiencing compliance and its implications, but it took a long time for me to realize this. I did not want others to feel lost like me, so I needed to make sure others felt connected, valued, and important. This has helped me in my professional life in so many different ways. Constantly connecting with others gave me access to other departments. It allowed me to understand other parts of the business and how each entity connects to each other and to the whole.

It allowed me to break down the silos and help create more collaborative spaces across the organization. I became the "executive whisperer," helping leaders see perspectives that may have eluded them outside the ivory tower. I created psychological safety for staff, nurtured my EQ, and became a mentor across all levels. As positive as this sounds, these were still the fruits of people-pleasing, not authenticity.

Ten years ago, something broke open. I could not keep performing myself into invisibility—not for one more dinner, not for one more performance review, especially not in front of my sons. They were watching me disappear, learning to do the same.

WHAT I GAINED FROM STOPPING COMPLIANCE

I walked away from a long-term marriage because I had found that I had perfected the art of compliance, wondering why I felt so alone beside him. Leaving felt like failing again, another path I could not finish. But this time, I understood the difference between failing at compliance and succeeding at honesty. I finally needed to do what was right for me, to live my life with authenticity.

I reconnected with my family, especially my dad, by being honest and authentic with him. We both opened up to each other. I told him what I had been too scared to say for 30 years—that I had spent my whole life trying to earn his approval after that weekend in college, how I always felt that I was not good enough. As we sat at the kitchen table, we both cried. He looked so sad and full of regret as he told me that all he wanted was to be there to support me, and that he has never been prouder of me and the woman I have become. I broke down, tears streaming down my cheeks. This honesty on both sides started to release me from the guilt I had built up in myself. This allowed me to devote intentional time to him. Soon after, we discovered that he had Lewy Body Parkinson's disease. He passed away a couple of years ago, but this reconnection after I stopped self-editing has opened up space for me to work through forgiving and healing, allowing me to be more authentic.

Every day, I intentionally work to be my true self while still keeping peace and harmony, which I continue to value. In reconnecting with my sister and mom and gaining their support, I am improving my communication skills and learning how to let go of being a pushover and start believing in myself the way others believe in me. I am finally being kind to myself. I have opened my eyes to see my now adult boys model this behavior successfully, giving me the permission I needed to continue living authentically. This is what has given me the freedom to keep growing without judgment.

I once believed that if I worked hard enough, followed the rules, and kept everyone comfortable, things would eventually fall into place. What I know now is that nothing truly aligns when you abandon yourself along the way. I am learning how to stay connected without self-erasure. How to value harmony without sacrificing honesty. How to live with less editing and more truth.

I am learning to catch myself now—in meetings when I am about to agree to something I do not want, in relationships when I feel the "no" rising in my throat. I pause. I ask: *Am I editing myself for comfort again?* Sometimes I still choose compliance, but only as a concession that I am prepared to make and *choose* to make. It is a choice, not a reflex. And that's where freedom begins, recognizing the old pattern and making the conscious decision to break it.

I do not have all this figured out. But I do know this: choosing myself no longer feels like failure.

My partner, who came into my life unexpectedly, reflects back to me the woman I am becoming: authentic, unedited, enough. It feels like coming home. It is where real belonging begins.

So, I will ask you what I have been asking myself: What would change if you stopped editing yourself for comfort? What connections might deepen if you chose authenticity over compliance? The answers will not come all at once. They did not come easily for me. But I promise you this: choosing yourself does not have to feel like failure. It can feel like coming home.

"Everything will line up perfectly when knowing and living the truth becomes more important than looking good." —Alan Cohen

ABOUT THE AUTHOR

SEEMA M. PATEL

Seema Patel, MBA, BSRC, RRT is a leader and clinician with over 30 years of experience in training, educating, mentoring, and facilitating organizational development. Seema helps people and teams grow to understand that meaningful connections between people, ideas, and communities are the foundation of transformational leadership. Seema fully extends her expertise in leadership development, change management, and organizational excellence with audiences committed to strengthening culture and performance.

Seema's work sits at the intersection of clinical practice, training, and quality, driven by a deep commitment to the people and processes that shape how care is delivered. She leads initiatives focused on accreditation, service excellence, and staff engagement. Having worked at the bedside and within systems, she understands how policy, culture, and people intersect in real time.

As a passionate advocate for inclusion and belonging, she leads employee engagement efforts and serves in professional communities dedicated to leadership talent development, public speaking and coaching. Across each space, her focus remains consistent: building bridges that strengthen both performance and culture.

A proud two-time graduate of Ohio State University, Seema embodies a commitment to lifelong learning, a value she has passed on to her two sons, who are also OSU alumni. She and her partner Russell live by the same principles she leads with: integrity, connection, and showing up for the people who matter. Guided by the belief that kindness is strength, not weakness, she leads with compassion and accountability.

For Seema, connection is not a leadership accessory. It's the truth.

CHAPTER TWO

SUMMER C. MARTIN

UNLEARNING WHAT ONCE WORKED

The year is 2019. I'm working in the tech industry in sales, experiencing heavy burnout and a sense of getting further away from the career path I'd designed for myself. I spent most of my counseling sessions coping with my fragile mental state and learning tools to help me navigate corporate microaggressions. I expected to be further up the corporate ladder. I felt like a failure.

I graduated from Southern University with confidence, ambition, and a belief that if I followed the rules, the system would reward me. I did what I was told to do: earned the degree, completed internships, joined professional organizations, showed up polished and prepared. When I moved to Dallas, I was certain opportunity would meet me halfway. I assumed job offers would rain down on me, or at least arrive steadily.

On paper, I was impressive. Phone interviews went beautifully — this was a mandatory step before video chat. Recruiters were enthusiastic. I was articulate, prepared, qualified. But something interesting would happen the moment I showed up in person. I could feel the shift before it was ever said out loud. The pause. The look. The polite surprise.

"Oh… you're Summer."

That sentence landed heavier than it should have. My heart would sink in those moments because I knew what it meant: *You didn't know I was Black.* Typically, after these moments, I'd give myself a pep talk in the car to ease the tension of rejection. I'd look at myself in the visor mirror and say, *Summer, no matter what, you are the shit and deserve all you strive for.* I was encountering an invisible barrier I hadn't been prepared for: the unspoken assumptions placed on a Black woman entering corporate America. I only knew that something kept closing right as I reached for it.

For two years post-graduation, I pieced together temp roles. Short-term assignments. In-between work. I told myself it was just part of the journey, that momentum would come. But privately, I was confused and frustrated. I had done everything "right." Where the hell was my dream job? Where was the salary I'd been promised? The one I was told would follow my efforts and excellence.

That's when the old script cracked — the one that said merit alone guarantees access, that talent always rises cleanly to the top, that bias is an exception, not a feature.

That realization didn't make me bitter, but it did wake me up. And once I saw the script for what it was, I couldn't unsee it.

WHAT I WAS REWARDED FOR THAT NO LONGER FIT

I'd be asked to join focus groups or committees at work to help inform leadership on business unit change initiatives. I thought these extracurricular activities would help me advance within the system. I felt honored to be asked. What I didn't yet understand was that being invited into the room and being positioned to move forward from it were two very different things.

There was one focus group assembled to generate new ways to expand revenue within an existing client base vertical. Leaders, senior reps, an executive sponsor — all energized by possibility.

When it was my turn, I proposed hosting live information sessions featuring current clients. Not scripted testimonials, but moderated conversations about how our services had strengthened their strategy and operations.

"I can host it," I said. "Hearing it from clients will carry more weight than hearing it from us." Heads nodded. A few reps voiced support. Our executive champion called it compelling.

I left that meeting feeling something I hadn't felt in a while: seen. Not just as a body filling a seat, but as someone with something worth building. I let myself believe this was the kind of moment that opened doors.

The following week, I asked my manager if I could partner with marketing to begin logistics. They asked me to schedule time to discuss details. I did. The meeting was later canceled due to an urgent matter.

I followed up again. No response. Weeks passed.

I sat with that silence longer than I should have. I kept telling myself it was timing, that the idea hadn't died, it had just stalled. I followed up one more time before I finally let it go — not because the idea lacked merit, but because I'd started to recognize something I didn't have language for yet.

The room had rewarded my participation. But advancement required sponsorship. And that was not being offered.

What stung wasn't the rejection — it was the clarity. I had been performing all the right moves inside a game that had different rules for me. And no one was going to tell me that directly. I had to feel my way to the realization myself, one unanswered email at a time.

THE COST OF STAYING COMFORTABLE

By the time I was a few years into corporate life, a pattern had formed. I didn't stay anywhere longer than two years. At the time, I framed it as ambition, growth, opportunity. And yes, often it was about the money.

But I wasn't building. I was repositioning.

I stayed in commercial real estate longer than I should have, believing I was investing in something that would pay off. When it didn't, I left for tech. I called it evolution. In hindsight, it was reaction.

The harder question — the one I kept avoiding — was whether any of these moves were actually mine. Was I building something meaningful, or just adjusting to the inner workings of a system that kept showing me its limits?

I didn't sit with that long enough to answer it honestly. Motion felt like progress, and as long as I kept moving, I didn't have to confront how far I'd drifted from who I set out to become.

Staying comfortable had a cost. Each move helped me survive. None of them helped me grow.

I didn't fully see that until everything stopped.

WHAT UNLEARNING ACTUALLY FEELS LIKE (NOT THE SOCIAL MEDIA VERSION)

Unlearning doesn't feel like a breakthrough montage. It feels like grief mixed with relief.

For me, unlearning became real during the pandemic. When the world slowed down, the noise quieted enough for me to hear my own discomfort clearly. I began asking myself what I was still carrying simply because it once worked, not because it still served me.

It was subtle and unsettling. Unlearning meant questioning beliefs I had built my life around. It meant releasing identities that had earned me approval. But it was also freeing. Unloading old expectations created space. Space for curiosity. Space for rest. Space for new ways of leading and living.

Unlearning isn't passive.

It's an active decision to stop rehearsing scripts that no longer match my values. It's choosing discomfort now instead of resentment later.

What I've learned is this: Learning adds. Unlearning liberates.

THE TENSION I STILL LIVE INSIDE OF AND THE POWER OF BOTH/AND

I live in a both/and space, allowing room for natural tensions. I've learned to recognize when I'm facing a problem to be solved and when I'm living inside a polarity to manage. An active polarity for me is the one between Appreciate What Is and Desire More. I honor and appreciate parts of the old script because some of it did protect me. It helped me survive. It taught me resilience, adaptability, and awareness.

At the same time, I am committed to rewriting what no longer aligns while desiring more.

Growth doesn't require erasing who I was. It requires discerning what to carry forward and what to release. This tension is not a flaw. It's evidence of consciousness.

WHAT I NOW KNOW ABOUT LEADERSHIP, HUMANITY, AND CHANGE

Leadership is not performance; it's example. What moves people isn't perfection, it's presence. People don't follow titles. They follow integrity, energy, and action.

We become more receptive to change when we lead with an open heart and mind. I challenge the idea that you can't change due to age or an inherent inability to shift. It's up to us to decide whether we believe we're worthy of more.

THE MYTH I HAD TO LET DIE

The belief that hard work always pays off came from my first and most influential example of success: my mother. I watched her career in education evolve from teacher's aide to area director for the Los Angeles County Office of Education. At the time, I didn't understand the full scope of her climb or the obstacles she navigated. What I saw was progress, stability, and respect.

She was consistently promoted over time. She worked from home long before it became normalized. I often went to work with her. To me, she embodied what success looked like. And without realizing it, I absorbed the myth that effort leads to reward — that if you show up, work hard, and do the right thing, the system will meet you with opportunity.

That belief protected me for a while. It gave me hope, direction, and a sense of control. But it began to unravel as I tried to launch my own career. The promised outcomes didn't materialize. The path didn't open the way I expected it to.

Still, I held onto the myth longer than I should have. I told myself to just keep going. *You're on your way to the C-suite.* I stayed in motion, convinced momentum would eventually turn into arrival.

The cost of that belief was subtle but significant. I spent years running on the same wheel, mistaking endurance for progress. Letting that myth die didn't mean rejecting effort. It meant releasing the lie that effort alone guarantees access.

WHAT NO ONE WARNS YOU ABOUT UNLEARNING

What surprised me most about unlearning was how freeing it felt. Letting go of ideas, traditions, and beliefs that no longer served me created a sense of lightness I didn't know I was missing. There is power in saying no to a way of thinking, especially one you were taught not to question.

But unlearning also came with loss, and no one really talks about that part. I lost time. Years spent trying to win at a game that was never designed for me to succeed. I lost trust in my own instincts for a while, outsourcing my sense of direction to systems and expectations that didn't have my best interest in mind.

What didn't immediately feel empowering was the forgiveness required. I had to extend grace to myself for believing I was behind, off track, or somehow wrong. I'm still practicing releasing my need to always have a plan or definitive answers.

Unlearning taught me that there isn't one guaranteed path to success. The work isn't to control the lesson, but to stay open enough to receive it.

HOW THIS CHANGED THE WAY I DEFINE SUCCESS

Success used to mean titles and paychecks. The bigger the title, the closer I thought I was to arrival.

That definition no longer works for me.

I stopped chasing metrics that required constant comparison — watching what others were doing, measuring my progress against timelines that weren't mine. That game was exhausting.

Today, I define success differently. I measure it by my mental state. By whether I feel grounded, inspired, and energized by the work I'm doing. I pay attention to whether my work creates impact, not just output.

Success now includes alignment, sustainability, and meaning. It looks like work that honors who I am and who I'm becoming. It looks like freedom to evolve.

That shift didn't make my goals smaller. It made them truer.

THE DIFFERENCE BETWEEN ENDURANCE AND GROWTH

Endurance has always been something I prided myself on. I know how to face adversity. I know how to push through. For a long time, that ability was praised — by others and by me.

I worked in tech sales at the same company for eight years before I walked away. Once removed from the environment, I could see what those years had cost me. I made good money. But the culture cost me more.

Sales carried a familiar energy — part fraternity, part good-ol'-boy hierarchy. Territories and pet projects weren't always assigned by merit. They flowed toward those leadership favored.

During one of our bootcamps, a senior leader stood in front of the room speaking about resilience. Mid-sentence, he looked toward me and said, "You're not the only one here who knows what it feels like to experience discrimination."

The room went still.

No one had mentioned discrimination. No context had been set. The comment hovered, undefined.

At the time, another rep (a white woman dating a Black man) was in our group, something he happened to know. His statement felt like projection, an attempt to equalize experiences without understanding them.

Heat rose in my chest. Instead of staying quiet, I responded evenly, "If we're sharing personal context, my fiancé is white."

A few nervous laughs followed. He shifted and moved on.

What stayed with me wasn't the awkwardness. It was the assumption — that proximity equals lived experience, that a vague nod to discrimination signaled awareness.

Moments like that accumulated. I told myself this was just sales culture. The money was good. I believed I could endure it long enough to rise within it.

I've since learned that endurance, when left unchecked, can quietly replace growth. It cost me more time. It cost me wellness.

Perseverance has power. But so does knowing when to stop — when the effort required outweighs the return.

Endurance keeps you standing. Growth moves you forward.

WHAT I NOW LISTEN FOR (INSTEAD OF FORCING CLARITY)

I used to believe clarity came from more information. More analysis. More thinking. But over time, I've learned that clarity shows up when I stop forcing it.

Now, when I need direction, I get still. I quiet the noise and remain open to what hasn't revealed itself yet.

What replaced certainty for me was discernment. Strengthening that muscle has eased my desire for constant reassurance. Instead of demanding answers, I listen for alignment. For energy shifts. For what feels expansive versus constricting.

Discernment doesn't eliminate uncertainty; it helps you move with it. And that has changed everything about how I make decisions, lead, and trust myself.

THE QUESTIONS I ASK NOW

I used to approach decisions by asking, *What should I do?* That question almost always pulled me outward, toward expectations, timelines, and other people's opinions. Over time, I learned that clarity doesn't come from urgency. It comes from alignment.

Now, the questions I return to are quieter and more internal. I ask myself where a choice aligns with my values. I listen to what my head is saying, and I make space for what my heart is signaling, even when the two aren't immediately in agreement.

These questions slow me down, and that's a good thing. They create a pause between impulse and action. Instead of reacting to noise, I use my values as a filter. They help me separate what's urgent from what's meaningful.

Clarity, I've learned, doesn't rush.

WHAT I PAY ATTENTION TO WHEN THINGS FEEL OFF

When something doesn't sit well with me, I no longer push through it the way I used to. I pause. I pay attention. I listen — not just intellectually, but physically.

My body has become one of my most trusted guides. It communicates before my mind has fully caught up. Tightness, restlessness, fatigue, a subtle sense of unease — these signals are information. For a long time, I ignored those cues, overriding them in the name of productivity or perseverance.

Now, I stop when something feels off. I ask what I am experiencing emotionally and physically, not just what I'm thinking. Awareness has changed how I respond. Instead of forcing myself forward, I give myself permission to reassess.

This doesn't mean every uncomfortable feeling is a stop sign. Growth can be uncomfortable. But there's a difference between healthy stretch and quiet resistance. I've learned to tell the difference by listening more carefully.

If something doesn't feel right mentally or physically, like a potential project, I don't proceed blindly. I pause, reflect, and recalibrate. That awareness has saved me from repeating old patterns and helped me move forward with greater integrity and trust in myself.

WHO I AM NOW AND WHAT I'M NO LONGER WILLING TO CARRY

If there's an invitation here, it's a quiet one: to notice what you're still carrying out of habit, and what might be ready to be set down. Not because you failed — but because you've grown.

I've put down the belief that there is a silver bullet to life's security. A single formula that guarantees stability, success, or certainty. For a long time, I carried the idea that if I followed the "right" steps in the "right" order, everything would work out exactly as promised.

What I hold differently now is grace. Grace for the unlearning. Grace for the years spent believing in a system that worked, until it didn't. There is no shame in having followed a formula that once served me. It taught me discipline, resilience, and awareness. I don't resent it. I honor what it gave me, and I allow myself to move forward without dragging it along.

I'm no longer chasing external validation to confirm who I am or what I'm worth. I'm also no longer willing to tolerate environments, expectations, or opportunities that require me to shrink or disconnect from myself. Alignment is no longer optional. It's foundational.

The leader I am choosing to be doesn't fit neatly into a label. I lead with curiosity, not certainty. I lead with an open heart and an open mind. I stay interested in growth — not as a destination, but as a practice. I pay attention to people, to nuance, and to what's unfolding beneath the surface.

I didn't become someone new through this process. I became more myself. More discerning. More grounded. More willing to stand in complexity without needing to resolve it immediately.

I'm still unlearning. Still practicing faith in the process. I remind myself often: I am where I'm meant to be, even when it's uncomfortable and unpredictable. This isn't a message from the mountaintop. It's a note from my path.

ABOUT THE AUTHOR

SUMMER C. MARTIN

Summer C. Martin is a leadership advisor, organizational development consultant, and author whose work centers on unlearning, change, and the human side of leadership in systems that reward performance over presence. She helps individuals and organizations navigate complexity by examining not just what needs to change, but who they are becoming in the process.

With a career spanning commercial real estate, technology, and consulting, Summer has spent more than two decades inside systems that reward endurance, proximity, and performance. Her work is shaped by firsthand experience navigating corporate cultures, leadership dynamics, and the unspoken rules that "quietly" govern access, advancement, and belonging.

Summer approaches leadership as a human practice before it is a performance metric. She believes change does not begin with strategy alone, but with awareness, integrity, and the courage to unlearn what once worked. Through coaching, facilitation, and advisory work, she supports leaders who are ready to move beyond performative change and toward practices that are sustainable, values-aligned, and honest.

Her writing explores the tension between endurance and growth, certainty and discernment, and the quiet decisions that shape our lives and leadership over time. Rather than offering formulas or prescriptions, Summer invites reflection, encouraging readers to question inherited scripts, listen more closely to themselves, and lead with greater presence and intention.

She lives and works in Plano, Texas with her husband and adorable Scottish Terrier, Charlie. Summer remains committed to work that honors humanity, complexity, and the ongoing "imperfect" practice of becoming.

CHAPTER THREE

M.C. TYLER

RUNNING ON EMPTY

Ding, ding. My email was pinging back to back. I had an important client meeting coming up that I was preparing a creative deck for. *Ding, ding*. People were asking how much I had left to do. Was there anything they could do to help me move things along? My time was dwindling. I've been known to procrastinate here and there, just as much as any other creative person, but this time was different.

I had done the pre-work needed to have this presentation in a solid place. I made sure to prepare, but it was so much work to do with so little time. Scrambling to get this deck put together, I had to pull in images from messy desktop folders and make sure all the text was in alignment in the presentation. Nothing vastly different than I had done before. This was my general approach to creative work. Timing was always in short supply. I constantly moved at 1000 miles per hour. So this wasn't new to me, but this feeling in my body was something different. There was this intense feeling inside of my chest that started to swell up.

Everything in the room started to feel like it was on a tilt. It felt like my head was throbbing, and I couldn't focus on my thoughts. But I had to, because I had to get this deck out the door. I had made a whole identity out of being the person who could push through anything. The more I worked, the more I began to sweat and feel sharp pains in my stomach. So I decided to do what any logical person would decide to do: stand up to do the work. No, not taking a break to check on myself. I started thinking, "Maybe I just need to get out of this sitting position. Yeah, that'll do the trick." It did not. I put my computer on my standing desk and continued cranking out the work. That was when I started to feel dizzy. It felt like the room was starting to spin.

"I can't focus on that right now. I have to focus on the work," I told myself. I ignored all the warning signals my body was giving me and kept working. But the more I ignored it, the more my body shut down on me. I put my hand over my stomach, taking shallow breaths, trying to gather all the racing thoughts so I could finish the client presentation. The more I worked, the worse that feeling got. At some point, I realized that I could barely see what was in front of me. I sat on the floor next to my desk, knees to chest. Forcing myself to take slow, intentional, deep breaths. I started to think it was working, but it wasn't. Everything I was feeling just intensified. I ran to the restroom. I was sick to my stomach by this point. I lay on the cold floor because it was the only thing giving me any relief. Would you believe that—on this cold floor, dizzy, sweating, sick to my stomach—I was still listening out for the *ding ding* of my email? I continued placing designs and images where they needed to go and making sure things were set up correctly.

Completely disregarding the pain that I was feeling, mentally and physically, I had that client presentation in the bathroom, lying on the floor. I thought absolutely nothing of it. I thought that the whole sequence of events was normal. That everyone functioned like that. In my mind, that's what made a "good employee." You had to care about the job more than you cared about your well-being.

But what I didn't realize was that that exact mindset is the fastest way to get you into early retirement. Not the sitting-on-a-beach retirement—the type of vacation you never come back from. It's not sustainable. Did I get the deck out? Yes. It was actually a really good presentation. I defaulted to performance and pushed forward to execute the job at a high level. But what I didn't know was that that moment would have a lasting effect on how my body and brain worked. It would lead to a struggle with depression, anxiety and massive panic attacks.

Now don't get me wrong—those struggles had been there for a long time prior, but that experience triggered something for me. It opened the door for all the things I had been ignoring through the years. It would take years and a lot of therapy to identify what I was going through. See, I thought that I was just being weak. I thought that my body wasn't doing what I told it to do. That it wasn't executing at the highest level that I know it could.

But after some time in therapy really sitting with and accepting my feelings, I was able to realize my body was yelling at me to stop. It was telling me that we were tired. I had nothing left in the tank. I had used and abused all the energy that I had. That I was like a car with no gas, no fluid, but I was still trying to drive it cross-country. I couldn't even start it up anymore. My body wouldn't allow me to move forward. Which at the time I was pretty upset about. But now I can appreciate it because my body knew better than I did. It knew that if we kept functioning at that level, we would break something we couldn't fix. I would stop and never be able to start up again. It was the result of years of learning how to override myself.

THE MAKING OF A "GOOD" EMPLOYEE

By the time the pandemic hit, I had already spent years working without taking any real breaks. I went from high school to art school, art school to interning, then straight into working full time at an agency. There was no breathing room, and that pace taught me to value myself by how much I could carry without breaking.

I stepped into a business that had a certain level of not caring about how people actually functioned outside of work. One year, I caught a really bad case of the flu and had to take myself to the emergency room. While I was stretched out in a hospital bed trying to catch my breath, my phone kept ringing with work notifications. They knew I was sick, but the work was the priority. I learned that whatever I had going on personally was not supposed to interfere with the work. That kind of thinking did not just shape how I handled that moment. It shaped how I understood work altogether.

Because of that, I never really had the opportunity to learn how to work in a healthy way. The job was always to focus on what needed to get done. Somewhere in that, I started to associate goodness with self-denial, responsibility with endurance, and strength with silence.

WHEN EVERYTHING SUDDENLY STOPPED

The pandemic was a tricky thing. It was the first time in my entire life that I was forced to stop. Forced to self-reflect on the person I had become, I paused and asked myself, *Am I actually doing okay?* I had to look in the mirror and realize I had worked so hard, there were years that had gone by that I didn't even remember. I went from this daily routine of waking up, brushing my teeth, throwing my clothes on, driving downtown, working in an office from 9 to 6, sometimes 8, then getting back to my car, driving home, grabbing something to eat, going to bed, then doing it all over again the next day.

Next thing I know, I'm waking up and deciding whether or not I'm even going to put clothes on for the day and open my computer to talk to people through a screen. This was the first time I had ever worked from home. My entire career to that point, I had worked physically in an office. So not only am I stopping my body and my mind, now I'm also isolated from seeing people every day.

I will never forget the day we were sent home because of the pandemic. We were all in the office doing our daily things. Working together, chatting, just being normal.

At this point, we had heard whispers of this sickness going around. We were all gathered in the kitchen talking, and one of the higher-ups walked up to us and in this matter-of-fact way said, "Hey, pack y'all's stuff and go home." We were all confused looking at each other like,

"What do you mean, 'go home'?" He looked at us and said, "Pack all your things. Go home. I don't know when we'll be coming back." I remember thinking how weird that conversation was. Like he knew something we didn't.

We spent the rest of that afternoon packing up our desks, computers, and clearing out our cubbies. I don't know why but I packed up everything I had brought to the office. Something about it felt permanent. And, lo and behold, I never went back to that office. What I didn't know was that leaving the office would also mark the beginning of a completely different relationship with work.

FACING MYSELF FOR THE FIRST TIME

That shift lasted far longer than any of us expected. Years later, I would still be working from home even after getting hired by a different agency. I hated working from home when we first transitioned. But now, as the person I am today, I realize that was because at some point I had to face myself day to day. I couldn't hide behind the busy schedule, being on calls, or meetings with people in person every day. I couldn't speed past my feelings. I had to stop, look myself in the face, and realize I wasn't okay. That I was allowing my life to slip by just to overwork myself to become the person I thought I was supposed to be.

When you aren't taught to care for yourself, it really doesn't register in your mind. You start thinking caring for yourself is a negative, not a positive. As if it slows you down from doing what you need to do. But I hit my breaking point mentally during that pandemic. Once the panic attacks started, I couldn't stop them. I could barely get on calls without hyperventilating right before. I did my best to muscle through because I thought that that's what a Black woman does. I grew up being unintentionally taught that you aren't supposed to feel anything.

You keep going no matter what's in front of you. You never let anybody see you sweat. That's what makes us "strong." The belief is that as hardships come, you throw them in a box, you put them on a shelf, and you continue to do the thing. All of the representations of being a Black woman in my life reinforced these ideas. You take care of your family, you do the work, you show up for your friends and literally everybody else except yourself. You never ask yourself, *Am I okay?* And nobody around you feels the need to ask you that either. So you begin to believe that this is how you're supposed to function. I wasn't just acting strong. I believed I had to be the strong one. Not only is it not how you're supposed to function, it's not sustainable. You will come to a stop eventually. For me, that gap of time during the pandemic was what I needed to stop and realize I was more than just what I could create. That every part of me needed care and tending to.

Reducing myself to just what I could output was a disservice to myself. Don't get me wrong—I was producing at a very high level when it comes to creative. I've always exceeded expectations when it came to making art. But there came a point where I thought that was all I was. I thought, "I'm a great person because I can produce at a high level." But during that self-reflection period, I could no longer produce the way I was used to. I had to really come to terms with the idea of production not equaling the value of who I was. I had to realize I was way more than that. I knew how to measure my output, but not how to value myself outside of it.

If I were to map out who I was on a piece of paper, it would be my name in the middle of the page in a circle with a couple of lines coming from it going towards painting, drawing, illustrating and designing. The things I did, but not who I was. Now, that map looks completely different. I would still have my name at the center of a page with a circle around it, then it would have multiple lines coming from it going towards my physical health, mental health, family, friends, relationships, kindness, empathy and so on. All these pillars are what make me the person that I am—way more than just what I can produce.

I have to factor in all these parts of me to get to the source of the creator in me. I also had to realize all those building blocks are at different phases of the journey. I had to nurture each of them differently for me to be able to produce the work that I wanted to. I had to check in to make sure that each part of me was excelling at its own pace because if one part of me was off, the producer side of me suffered. In learning to pay attention to myself, I also began to notice what had been missing in the way I had been led.

WHAT REAL LEADERSHIP LOOKS LIKE

Earlier in my career, I can't recall a time when I had a manager who asked me how I was doing and meant it in a genuine way. Not just as another way of asking whether the work was done. Questions like, "How do you feel" had never really been asked to me before. Now that I was in this place of personal struggle, it affected how I showed up at work. I had a greater appreciation for what a simple question like, "How are you holding up?" could mean to a person. How when you check on what people have going on in their lives, you're having a positive impact on their work.

This starts with being aware enough to notice that someone is being more quiet than normal in meetings. Taking that as an opportunity to message someone or take them aside and ask, "Are you doing okay? You seemed quiet today." There was a time when I started to outwardly show that I was personally having a hard time. I stopped showing up to group connects and all-around seemed disconnected from everyone and everything. The panic attacks I was secretly having became more frequent. I finally broke down and asked my manager at the time to have a quick meeting with me. We sat down and she kindly asked me, "What's been going on with you? You seem distant." Before I could speak, I broke down crying.

As best I could in between the tears, I told her all that had been happening in my life at that time. I said to her two simple words, "I'm struggling." She assured me that struggling was okay and that I didn't need to apologize for taking time for myself. That conversation highlighted the way I had been led before versus now. Moments like this build people's trust in you as their leader. Healing changed how I worked, but it also changed how I saw people. Once I stopped complying with the old identity, I became more capable of real connection, with myself and with others. That shift also made me pay closer attention to the people around me and the ways work can quietly wear a person down.

THE COST OF IGNORING OURSELVES

I used to work with a man named James who came in bright and early every morning. James was quiet but kind. Every day was the same routine for me. I would get off the elevators, walk through the double glass doors, make a right past the kitchen and throw up my hand to wave at James. He would quickly throw up his hand back and give me a quick grin before he immediately went back to staring at his computer. He would be in before everybody, and would stay past everyone leaving for the day. It never failed—every time I arrived at the office, he would have already been there for a couple hours.

One day, I walked into the building and he wasn't there. The first day in the years I had been working there that I could recall him not being there before me. We were later told that he'd had a massive stroke, and that he'd be hospitalized for a bit of time. Roughly a couple of months later, he was back working in the office. After all that he had been through, he felt that he needed to be back at work finishing the things he had left behind. We didn't think much of it; we were just happy to have him back. We spoke to him, we laughed, and we went about our day as normal.

Maybe a couple weeks later, we came in, and he was gone again. I thought maybe he had rushed coming back to work so soon and needed a little more time to rest his body. Around lunchtime, an email went out to the agency that stated he'd had a heart attack and died.

Apparently there's a window of time where your risk of having a devastating medical event increases after having something as serious as a stroke. I was completely caught off guard. The thought of never seeing him again really started to sink in. I went to the kitchen and sat at one of the booths to gather my thoughts and realized something else was happening. Everyone was going about their day like nothing had happened. No one offered letting us take the rest of the day to grieve the loss of someone we saw every day for years. It was business as usual.

You may get lucky and have a manager that's caring and considerate of what you have going on. But if you don't, you have to make time to care for your mental and physical health. Be excellent in all that you do, but know that what you do isn't more important than who you are.

At the end of the day, work will end. Who you are will last much longer for those you've interacted with. You don't need some grand reason for feeling the way you feel or some medical diagnosis to make it matter. It matters just because. Take a daily inventory of what's affecting who you are and prioritize getting the help you need to get through the inevitable hardships of life. It's not a question of if difficulty will come—it's a matter of when. And even knowing that, I still resisted getting the kind of help I needed for a long time.

BECOMING SOMEONE NEW

After everything I had been through, therapy was still my very last resort. Only after being at my very lowest did I consider therapy to be an option. The bottom is a real place. You will drive yourself crazy trying to fix a problem when you don't have the knowledge to identify the root of the issue. Therapy gave me the awareness of why I was struggling in certain areas. I thought knowing the problem would automatically shift what I was going through. I didn't realize knowing that I needed to adjust wasn't the same as actually doing the work to change my life. It was just information. I had to determine what I was actually going to do with that information. And part of that meant accepting that awareness was only the beginning, not the end.

There's no ending where you go to therapy for a while and all the things in your life are better forever. You string together a bunch of small wins until one day you look up and you realize you're a different person. People start to say you seem different to them, even though they can't pinpoint what changed. You'll have a moment when you look into the mirror and no longer see the person you used to be, but you see all of the possibilities of who you can become.

That's the win.

I never could have expected the great sense of relief I would feel the first time I chose to not push through the chaos. Not only was it relief—it was the realization that the world didn't end. People weren't angry with me not having anything left to give. They respected it.

Becoming someone new did not mean becoming perfect. It meant becoming honest. Committing to no longer measuring myself by only what I could carry, create or survive. Learning that care, rest, honesty and having limits did not make me weak, it made me real.

For years, I believed pushing through everything was what made me strong. What I understand now is that strength sometimes looks like stopping. It looks like listening when your body says, "Enough." It looks like admitting when you are struggling and allowing yourself to be cared for.

That day on the bathroom floor felt like failure. Now I understand it was the moment my body finally refused to let me keep pretending I was okay. Listening to that refusal changed everything.

ABOUT THE AUTHOR

M.C.
TYLER

M.C. Tyler is is an illustrator, designer, and creative leader whose work is rooted in storytelling, strategy, and the power of art to connect people to something deeper.

A graduate of the Art Institute of Dallas, she has spent more than a decade working in marketing and advertising, growing from Junior Art Director to Creative Director while helping shape work for major brands including ExxonMobil, Frito-Lay, and the NBA.

But long before the titles and brand work, M.C. Tyler was a young artist teaching herself how to draw and discovering that art could be a place of peace. That early love for creating has stayed with her through every season of her life, shaping not only the work she makes, but the way she moves through the world.

Her journey through corporate creative spaces has given her a unique perspective on leadership, identity, and growth. Each experience has helped mold her into the thoughtful, grounded leader she is today. As a founder of Maeart Creative, she continues to use her voice and experience to encourage others to grow in both their creativity and confidence.

M.C. Tyler creates with heart, leads with intention, and believes the stories that shape us are often the ones worth telling most.

PART II

THE COST OF STAYING QUIET

Courage, Conviction, and Speaking Truth in Leadership

"Our lives begin to end the day we become silent about things that matter."

—Dr. Martin Luther King Jr.

CHAPTER FOUR

BRIANA BROWN, M.Ed

WHEN SILENCE IS NO LONGER AN OPTION

Before you step into this space, take a breath. Get centered. My hope is that you leave this chapter better than you entered it. Whether through one sentence, one story, one lesson, or one quiet realization after you close the book. The words ahead will matter most when you're ready to receive them. Timing shapes understanding. So step in with curiosity, courage, and compassion—for yourself first, and then for others.

Let's begin.

TOWN HALL: HERE WE GO AGAIN

During my college years, a race-based incident escalated into a campus-wide town hall. I attended with a mixture of rage, confusion, and apprehension. I expected to learn from the institution, from my peers, and from the dialogue itself. What I did not expect was that the most significant lesson would be about myself.

I attended a predominantly white institution where African-Americans comprised roughly six percent of the student body. That number shaped daily life in visible and invisible ways. It meant heightened visibility in classrooms and meetings. It meant feeling both hyper-seen and unseen at the same time. It meant knowing that when something racial happened, even if it was not directed to me personally, it landed close enough to feel personal.

By that point, I held a leadership role in one of our campus organizations. Leadership in that environment carried an unspoken expectation: when race entered the room, leaders of color would interpret it, contextualize it, and respond to it. The responsibility extended beyond position; it became emotional work. You were expected to translate pain into something digestible.

The incident that prompted the town hall was brazen: a white fraternity required its pledges to wear blackface. This was not an obscure history. The harm was documented. The symbolism was unmistakable. I had encountered microaggressions before, questions about belonging, surprise at competence, subtle distancing in academic spaces, but this was public and undeniable. The campus could not pretend it had not happened.

I stepped into the dimly lit ballroom, my body tight and shoulders rigid. Chairs shifted and rustled as people found their seats, and the low hum of side conversations mingled with the faint scent of worn carpet and paper. I remember thinking, *Do I have the energy for this?* I also knew that if I did not speak, I would replay my silence long after the meeting ended. At the time, I did not have formal language for systemic bias or institutional accountability. What I had were feelings—layered, urgent, heavy. The feelings came in waves:

- The burden of being the token.
- The pressure to teach others why their actions caused harm.
- The responsibility to be the "bigger person."
- The fatigue of repeatedly taking one for the team.
- The discomfort of standing in front of truth while others debated whether it was truth at all.

The room was meant to be a reflective space. Yet reflection requires a willingness to sit with discomfort and to be accountable for what it might reveal, and not everyone arrived with that willingness. I overheard someone ask, "What's the big deal with blackface?" The question was casual, so casual that it intensified the weight I was already carrying. In that moment, the burden felt even heavier. Casual harm signals cultural permission.

When the opportunity to speak arose, I hesitated. My heart raced. I did not prepare a speech. I worried about being dismissed as emotional. I worried about saying too much or not enough. I also understood that silence would not protect me from discomfort. It would only relocate it inward.

I asked for the microphone and took a deep breath. Instead of delivering a speech, I led a brief exercise:

- Stand if you had heard about the incident before today.
- Stand if you have ever, perhaps unintentionally, caused harm to someone.
- Stand if you have ever been on the receiving end of harm.
- Stand if you know someone standing here.

With each prompt, more people rose. By the final question, the entire room was on its feet. For a moment, the room felt charged and alive. Bodies moving, shifting, acknowledging truths both spoken and unspoken. The quiet side conversations had disappeared, replaced by the quiet weight of presence. In that instant, I felt a shift within myself: relief, recognition, and the heavy awareness of shared responsibility. The room itself seemed to lean into the moment, holding both the pain and the possibility of understanding.

The visual shifted the energy. No one was isolated. No one could pretend harm was abstract. Accountability became collective. In that moment, I understood something I could not yet articulate: awareness changes posture. Once harm is visible, neutrality becomes participation.

That town hall marked my first conscious recognition of a pattern I would encounter repeatedly: progress followed by resistance; resistance followed by recalibration; recalibration followed by re-engagement. The cycle felt predictable even then. *Here we go again.*

Over time, I learned that this cycle is not accidental. Systems protect themselves. When confronted with truth, they often respond with delay, minimization, procedural distraction, or emotional deflection. The labor of pushing forward frequently falls on those most impacted. Yet repetition builds resilience. Through experience, discernment sharpens. Courage becomes practiced rather than performative. I learned to anticipate resistance without being surprised by it.

In that town hall, something shifted in me. I began to see that while I could not control the system, I could influence the moment. I could interrupt silence. I could shift energy. I could require acknowledgement.

That realization would follow me into every room thereafter.

THE WORKPLACE PATTERN: AND IT CONTINUES

Years later, I found myself working for a small nonprofit advancing social justice through science. The organization was growing rapidly, a startup in nonprofit terms, and navigating the inevitable "growing pains" that come with scaling. In this phase, nonprofits often engage in strategic reflection: aligning daily operations with mission, evaluating impact, and course-correcting when work drifts from values. But misalignment can be subtle, pervasive, and exhausting.

I had been noticing subtle signals of misalignment for some time. A comment in a meeting that minimized someone's contribution. A procedural barrier that seemed unnecessary but slowed certain my peer minority colleagues. Small inequities that passed unchallenged. Each incident alone might have seemed insignificant, but together they formed a persistent pattern of harm, shaping the daily experience of those around me. I felt the need to brace myself, ready for when the pattern would inevitably surface in a way I couldn't ignore. And one day, it did.

We were preparing promotional materials for a labor policy panel. My role was to post content on social media, a task that required accessing an image file in Canva. No approval was necessary, and the file had already been given a thumbs-up by the highest approver. I opened it, tilted my head, squinted at the screen, and looked around the room in disbelief. The illustration wasn't "innocuous." For me, labor policy meant laws, people, rights—not fields. Yet the image depicted fieldworkers in ways that evoked scenes reminiscent of slavery. My chest tightened. My stomach knotted. My mind raced: *Should I be the bigger person? Must I teach someone again? Am I going to have to carry this weight for the team once more?* The sender had intended it as "lighthearted," but to me, it landed like a shockwave, reopening old emotional wounds and reminding me how quickly harm could ripple through a system.

I spoke with my boss, expecting accountability. Before responding in the meeting, she "did research" and found out the image was from overseas and it was people working. Research to defend what we all knew was inappropriate. She said she would address it. Years later, she admitted she had not. She had hoped it would resolve itself. In her avoidance, others were harmed, harm shifted, and new patterns formed. The cycle was clear: harm does not disappear on its own. Ignoring it allows it to persist, morph, and spread.

Unchecked harm in the workplace is rarely dramatic. It unfolds quietly through hyper-scrutiny, unnecessary bureaucratic hoops, subtle sidelining, and repeated questioning of competence. I watched colleagues' voices dim, creativity fade, potential unrealized. I stepped in where I could: advocating for teammates, questioning unusual barriers, challenging inequitable hoops, and raising issues with leadership. But ultimately, the pattern forced choices. Two brilliant, capable Black women left the organization. My heart broke—I could not cover my peers from harm I felt like I let persist. So I stayed longer, absorbing fatigue, until I realized the harm was persistent, structural, and undeniable. Enough was enough.

Again, progress met resistance, recalibration, re-engagement. Now the system was a workplace, but the feelings were hauntingly familiar: exhaustion, moral tension, ambiguity, responsibility, the fatigue of educating others. Unlike college, I had more tools, perspective, and awareness to recognize patterns. Systems alone don't change—they require action.

Reflection became my tool. I remember sitting at my desk after a long day, jaw clenched, chest heavy, replaying the image and its ripple effects. I opened my notebook and began an exercise: writing immediately after each meeting or incident, capturing exactly what happened, what was said, what was left unsaid, and how people responded. I recorded moments when words didn't match actions, when harm was ignored, when expectations were unclear or unfair. Over time, patterns emerged. What had felt like isolated incidents were rarely isolated. They were structural, systemic, psychological, but now visible. The exercise forced me to confront a deeper truth: the missing element in these cycles was often me. My presence, my voice, my discernment, my courage. These patterns weren't just obstacles—they were opportunities to act differently.

Preparing for these cycles required intentionality. I developed strategies to prevent reactive exhaustion from dictating my response: mental rehearsals, accountability systems, frameworks for intervention. I began thinking not just about surviving, but thriving. How could I create a protective yet proactive posture? How could I influence outcomes without being consumed by fatigue or despair?

I started showing up differently. I became explicit about the values guiding my actions—fairness, accountability, dignity. Naming these values shifted conversations from personalities to responsibility. I was deliberate about who carried the work of change, ensuring the weight did not rest solely on those experiencing harm. I engaged allies intentionally, inviting colleagues with positional influence to ask questions, challenge patterns, and move work forward. I paused when necessary to protect my energy, recognizing that leadership sometimes means stepping back as well as stepping forward. Mentoring others became another tool. I shared lessons early so that those following would not carry what I had once carried alone. My mantra became clear: "Teach others early what I learned late."

Challenges began to feel different. They were no longer obstacles to endure. They became opportunities to exercise agency and practice intentional leadership. I learned to hold accountability and compassion at the same time: speaking clearly when systems failed while inviting others into the responsibility of repair. Mentoring amplified impact beyond my individual effort, reducing the cumulative fatigue that often accompanies these cycles. Slowly, the posture shifted. I was no longer simply reacting to harm. I was shaping how to respond to it—and, when possible, how to prevent it.

By the end of this phase, I had built a toolkit of awareness, resilience, strategic presence, community building, documentation, and reflection. This allowed me to respond to harm more intentionally and protect both myself and those around me. I could see patterns earlier, intervene more thoughtfully, and help others navigate the cycles with me. Yet even with these skills, I felt the limits of my own capacity. The work was still heavy, and I could feel how much more I needed: deeper clarity about my own responses, stronger support from others, and a better understanding of the internal patterns that kept pulling me back into the same dynamics. I had grown, but I also knew there was more to uncover, and there was more to learn about showing up in ways that were not only reactive, but purposeful and sustainable. I realized that the next step required turning inward, paying attention not just to the system around me, but to the system within me.

THE MIRROR: POWER IN THE PAUSE

Eventually, endurance alone was no longer sustainable. I had learned to navigate cycles of resistance, misalignment, and harm. I absorbed the impact, recalibrated, and moved forward. But survival was no longer enough. I wanted to understand the internal patterns that kept pulling me back into the same dynamics.

One executive coaching exercise demanded exactly that. Sit in front of a mirror. Several uninterrupted minutes. No distractions, no performance, just observation. At first, it felt almost trivial—*Is she serious?* I asked myself. But the longer I stayed, the heavier the quiet became. My jaw clenched, chest tight, hands itching to move. My instinct was to shift, adjust, or look away. Part of me wanted to escape. Another part knew I could not unsee what I was beginning to recognize. So I stayed.

In that stillness, the surprises came. I saw resilience, but also depletion. Courage, but also overextension. Strength had always been my default: when something went wrong, I stepped in; when systems faltered, I tried to repair them; when harm appeared, I absorbed the weight. And yet, face-to-face with myself, I felt the cost I had long ignored. My action had often come at the expense of rest, clarity, and presence. I realized how reflexively I moved before reflection. Action had been my armor, but without pause, it was quietly driving me toward burnout.

The mirror forced deeper questions: *Who am I? Who am I when there is no crisis to respond to? What do I stand for when I am not reacting? Who am I beyond intervention?* The answers weren't organized, but they were revealing. Reflection revealed patterns, where energy was depleted, where interventions could shift outcomes. Action became guided by insight rather than urgency. Reaction, I understood, was immediate, emotionally charged, and exhausting. Strategy, in contrast, required deliberation, grounding, and sustainability. That shift changed everything. Anger became information rather than impulse. Frustration became a signal for boundaries. Empathy no longer required self-erasure. Preparation replaced surprise. Strategy replaced exhaustion. "Here we go again" gradually became "I am ready."

For the first time, I felt the possibility of showing up intentionally at a deeper level. I could pause before stepping in, notice my own stance, and decide how to act with clarity and focus. I could discern when my presence would create impact, and when stepping back was a form of strength. I was beginning to separate my responsibility from the system's dysfunction. I was beginning to understand that endurance alone was not enough; I needed intentionality, self-awareness, and insight into my own internal dynamics.

Slowly, the posture shifted. I was no longer simply reacting to harm. I was shaping how to respond, and, when possible, how to prevent it. I realized it was time to disrupt the pattern, to step forward not just to survive, but to intentionally influence what came next.

SAME PATTERN, DIFFERENT POSTURE

When I look back, the arc is clear. A young undergraduate stepped forward in crisis. A professional navigated subtle, persistent misalignment. A reflective leader cultivated strategy through coaching and self-examination. Across contexts, the constant was agency. Patterns were structural, systemic, and psychological but not immutable. Growth is iterative and cumulative. Change requires courage paired with preparation.

What happens when we stop editing ourselves for comfort and choose connection over compliance or complacency? We speak up. We refuse silence. We show courageous presence.

The old version of me, the one entering that town hall, would have understood this: the weight of change does not rest on those who are harmed. Standing, speaking, showing up matters, even when the room feels heavy, resistant, or indifferent. A voice can be both mirror and lever, reflecting truth while moving others toward accountability. Years later, I live that truth every day. I lean into discomfort. I notice my posture, my breath, my energy. I refuse complacency. I act with clarity, courage, and accountability. I bring others along, sharing lessons early so they do not carry what I once carried alone.

Challenges are no longer obstacles to endure—they are opportunities to exercise agency, to claim leadership in the moment, to intervene before harm escalates. Accountability and compassion coexist. Action follows reflection. Presence becomes power.

And so we return to where we began: with a breath. Awareness precedes action. Reflection precedes strategy. Centering precedes intervention.

The cycles continue. Systems resist. Silence may seem easier. You cannot control the existence of the cycle, but you can control your posture within it. Choose connection over comfort. Take a deep breath. Speak. Stand. Act. Do what *you* can to change the shape of what comes next.

ABOUT THE AUTHOR

BRIANA
BROWN, M.Ed

Briana Brown (she/her) is a people-centered leader, strategist, and social justice advocate committed to building equitable, high-performing organizations. With more than a decade of experience across education, nonprofit management, and strategic consulting, she partners with mission-driven teams to design systems that align values with measurable impact.

Briana is passionate about supporting women, especially those from historically excluded communities, in navigating power, living in their truth, and leading with confidence. She believes leadership is less about title and more about alignment, courage, and community. Her approach blends strategic rigor with compassion, helping leaders pursue excellence without compromising equity or authenticity.

Grounded in academic training in educational psychology and biological sciences, Briana brings both analytical depth and a nuanced understanding of human behavior to her work. Her expertise spans HR strategy, performance management, mediation, compensation and benefits analysis, and organizational policy development. She translates bold vision into practical structures that make clarity possible and growth sustainable.

As a mother and justice-centered leader, Briana champions what she calls sustainable boldness. It is the practice of leading with integrity and ambition while remaining anchored in who you are. She creates spaces where hard conversations are not avoided, but navigated with intention. Because when women lead in their truth, organizations do more than perform. They transform.

CHAPTER FIVE

NAYSHONDRA MERCER, MA, CPC, ELI-MP

THE LION, THE BEAR, AND THE GIANT

"Something is broken in the human spirit, a fracture so deep that it convinces us to harm, exclude, and devalue one another as if we are not all connected." —Dominique Hollis, A Conscious Leadership Collective: Volume I: Leading From Within

Leading by design and not default is hardly an overnight phenomenon. To the contrary, it's a lifelong journey. One that is built moment by moment. It's unlearning, pivoting, and fighting against what you once knew to be true. It's hard-fought and hard-won battles that no one ever sees. Other times, it's on a public stage and the whole world watches. No matter your story, this leadership journey is the same. It's doing the uncomfortable thing. It's speaking up when you'd rather hide. It's going first when you'd rather opt out. It's speaking Truth to power when you'd rather comply. It's a journey that starts early and ends late. For some of us, as early as childhood. At least that's where my story began. Let me tell you about the time I fought the lion, the bear, and the giant.

THE LION

It was 1997 when my parents packed up our lives in Portage, Indiana, and relocated us to Columbia, South Carolina, where my mother was stationed at Fort Jackson. I had been partially raised in Charleston, South Carolina—my mother's hometown—so I was familiar with Southern pleasantries. I knew how to say "yes, ma'am" and "no, sir." I knew how to smile sweetly. To be seen and not heard. I was also well aware of South Carolina's history—its ties to the Klan, its public love affair with the Confederate flag, its role as the birthplace of the Civil War.

What I was not accustomed to was being asked, "Can I touch your hair?" Or the curiosity that masquerades as concern when classmates ask if I'm adopted. Or if my mother is White. Because how else could I explain being a lighter shade of Black than the rest of my family? And my personal favorite: the weekly letters sent home encouraging my parents to register for reduced school lunch.

We did not qualify. Yet week after week, my teacher sent those letters home anyway. Because in her mind, Black must mean poor.

At eight years old, I didn't fully grasp the weight of that assumption. But I recognized the tightness in my mother's jaw every time one of those letters hit the kitchen counter. She would exhale sharply, look at me, and say, "Tell your teacher we make too much money for reduced lunch."

"Yes, ma'am."

I delivered the message.

But did the letters stop?

No.

Instead, new letters joined them—complaints about me. Suddenly, I was no longer the shy, inquisitive, "gifted" student I had been in Indiana. In the South, I had developed a reputation. I was labeled condescending. Talkative. A problem. I was frequently sent to the guidance counselor for "behavior talks."

What my teacher did not see—or chose not to see—was the harassment happening right under her nose. As an Army Brat, I was always "the new girl," but never for too long. I was described as shy until one got to know me, then I would talk your head off and ask if you wanted to come over and play. But the South… Baby, the South was different! In the South I was made fun of because my hair was braided down neatly with pretty beads and my White peers couldn't understand why my hair "didn't move" like theirs. I was picked on for the way that I talked, which apparently "sounded White." And way too often I was told that I was "pretty for a Black girl." I knew something about that was off.

If you weren't aware, let me school you for a second: it's never a compliment to tell a person of color that they "speak proper" or that they "sound White." We speak English. That's not exceptional—it's expected. And it is not a novelty when a Black woman changes her hair. Nor is our beauty conditional. Black is not a disclaimer. Black is beautiful. Now, back to the story.

So when I was "othered," I was known to respond swiftly.

One afternoon during reading time, a classmate insulted me, yet again. I defended myself. Because when someone cut me with words, I cut back. My teacher only heard my rebuttal. She stopped the lesson, looked me dead in my eyes, and said in front of everyone, "Why are you so mean? That's why you don't have any friends."

Detention. Again.

The sounds of my peers laughing and playing outside felt louder when I was stuck inside replaying the scene, trying to figure out how I kept getting punished for what was done to me. At 36 years old today, I understand emotional regulation in ways second-grade Nayshondra did not. I can see how my reactions were what earned me consequences. But at eight? I just knew I was being treated differently and that I was the only one.

And that difference had a color.

So, I did what bold, confused little girls do. I forgot all about being seen and not heard and instead, I learned to defend myself. Not well, at first, but over time—I got better.

Being raised in the Church, I understood the Golden Rule: do unto others as you'd have them do unto you (Luke 6:31). So the treatment that I was receiving from my teacher and classmates confused me.

Was that how they wanted me to treat them, too?

Was I supposed to fight fire with fire?

Was I not to consider what Jesus would do? #IYKYK

At such a young age, I was hardly prepared to give my life for my enemy. But I was certainly on board with defending myself, standing my ground, and fighting back for a good cause like David did.

Yes, that David. The shepherd boy from 1 Samuel who would one day become king. The ancestor of Jesus. The one we quote when we talk about giants.

Before David ever faced Goliath, he faced a lion. And a bear.

When King Saul doubted his ability to take down the giant, David said: "When a lion or a bear came and carried off a sheep from the flock, I went after it… I struck it… I rescued the sheep from its mouth… The Lord who rescued me from the paw of the lion and the paw of the bear will rescue me from the hand of this Philistine." (1 Samuel 17:33–37)

David fought predators in private before he ever stood on a battlefield in public.

No applause.
No audience.
No crown waiting.
Just conviction.

In the same way, some of us learn to fight early. Not for recognition. Not for validation. But because something in our spirit refuses to bow to injustice.

Now, you might ask, "How can a child fight racism? What difference could you possibly make?"

Truthfully? I didn't know how. I was too young to recognize the giant that I was facing.
I just knew it was wrong.

I knew I was being treated differently than my White classmates. And that knowing was enough to make me resist. Enough to make me speak. Enough to make me disrupt what felt oppressive.

And yes—disruptive is exactly what they called me.
But anything that challenges an unjust system will always be labeled disruption before it is recognized as bravery.

That second-grade classroom was my lion.

And baby, I fought it.

THE BEAR

The year was 2020, and it felt like the entire world was on fire. On the outside, life kept moving. On the inside, I was anything but fine.

I was angry. Hurt. Exhausted. Tired of watching members of my community—men and women who looked like me—become hashtags and headlines after being unjustly murdered because of the color of their skin.

Ahmaud Arbery. George Floyd. Breonna Taylor.

Their names dominated the news for weeks. And they never left my heart.

At the time, I was working at the University of South Carolina, teaching through the College of Social Work. One day, a colleague posted something on social media that was insensitive, tone deaf, and, quite frankly, ignorant toward people who look like me. It was hatred thinly veiled as political support for the sitting president, and seeing it made my blood boil. I realized in that moment that staying silent was no longer an option.

I took action. I emailed this colleague directly and shared how her words caused harm—not only to me, but to her other Black and Brown colleagues who had graciously given up their office spaces to accommodate her during office renovations. I also carbon-copied our director, intentionally bringing visibility to the cognitive dissonance we were allowing within our organization.

To my surprise, our director, direct manager, and senior manager all reached out to commend my bravery and directness. They thanked me for saying what others felt but had not voiced. They encouraged me to have a one-on-one conversation with my colleague, which I agreed to do.

That conversation ended with us agreeing to disagree. I walked away proud—not because the conversation was comfortable, but because it was necessary. I chose action over avoidance. I stood my ground. I advocated for myself and for my community.

My decision to speak up created a ripple effect. It gave our director the permission he needed to address the injustices he, too, was witnessing. He started sending a weekly letter to the entire organization, openly acknowledging systemic inequities and calling for awareness, accountability, and change.

My heart was beating out of my chest when I hit "send," knowing that I had potentially jeopardized my job. But I didn't care.

Change doesn't happen in the dark; only when it is brought into the light. Through this experience, I learned a lesson I carry into every room: someone must go first. As a leader, I am committed to leading by example—no matter the size of the proverbial bear—because advocacy is not optional when harm is present.

Besides, the bigger they are, the harder they fall.

THE GIANT

The year was 2023 and life felt like a battlefield. I was on another healing journey following a breakup and learning new coping skills to support me after a two-week stabilization stay in the psychiatric hospital at the end of 2022; an experience I shared in the bestselling anthology, *Awareness Put Me On.* I was almost a year into my new role in multifamily property management, serving as the talent development specialist for a small company.

I was new to the industry, and even though my coaching and instructing skills were top-notch, the OGs wouldn't let me forget I was a newbie. As part of my new role, I'd reach out to the middle managers to offer my support and seek understanding of their current learning and development needs, only to be met with snide remarks about naivety and told that they didn't need my help.

I was shocked. I'd never been in a position where my support wasn't needed. After all, my role was in support services. But during meetings, I'd often be overlooked for comments and introductions—or excluded altogether. At every turn, I was reminded that I didn't know the ins and outs of multifamily, therefore, I couldn't possibly help the company with its learning and development needs.

Well, if you haven't noticed this about me yet, I am not easily shaken. So, I took the chastisement on the chin and started spending my spare time reading books on multifamily, attending trainings, and listening to podcasts—determined to catch up. And catch up I did! In less than a year, I'd closed the gap in my lack of knowledge, earned a promotion to talent development manager, and watched everything change. Now, not only was my input in meetings solicited and appreciated, but I was also being called on in rooms that I had not yet entered and asked to come in and present a workshop to address the company's interpersonal challenges.

But this was recognition that did not sit well with my new director. A beautiful, blonde-haired, blue-eyed woman more than 20 years my senior with an extensive 30+ year reputation in the industry. Our relationship started positively. Where she lacked knowledge in formal adult learning practices, I compensated. Where I lacked industry knowledge, she was a wealth of information. But our relationship suddenly took a turn for the worse.

I noticed the change in attitude when my director asked me for assistance with creating new training for the company. I agreed to help her and reviewed the training materials that she presented me with, noticing that this training was written on her own personal company letterhead. When I reviewed the materials, I realized the content was almost the identical to the curriculum I was already instructing.

When I presented that realization to my director, she tried to convince me that the content was completely different. I asked where those differences were and if she'd be willing to show me. She attempted to but soon noticed what I was alluding to: the content *was* the same. She was trying to deceive me into updating her own personal work. It no longer mattered that I was new to the industry, or that I was younger and Black. I'd made it clear that I knew what I was doing, and she wanted access. Now that we were on the same page, I informed my director that I would continue to use the content that we already had, and that I would not be altering her own personal content.

From that moment on I was her enemy and she began micromanaging me. I felt the hairs stand up on the back of my neck when I heard her calling me via Microsoft Teams every weekday at 9:00 a.m., on camera, to ensure that I was working. When she hosted a meeting and introduced everyone else on the call except me, I could feel my blood boiling beneath my shirt as I reminded myself not to show my irritation on my face. And my favorite: when I refused to work after-hours, she came after my character, stating that I wasn't a team player, I wasn't pulling my weight, and I was being manipulative.

That was where I drew the line.

Up until this point, I did not have a witness to what I was subjected to by my director, such as her microaggressions during one-on-one meetings, her overall cultural insensitivity, and the many times I sat quietly in a meeting, crying. But her comments regarding my character were expressed in a team meeting and our training manager was present. I knew then that it was time to act.

I sent an email. To her and to human resources (HR), and I carbon-copied the senior vice president (VP) of Operations, calling out her maltreatment and requesting an official meeting. The day of the meeting, all parties were present, and I was given the floor to begin. Being a woman of faith, I started the meeting by inviting wisdom into the room:

"I am a woman of deep faith. I was raised in and still serve in the Church. Now, that's not to make anyone uncomfortable, but just to give context as to why we are here today. The Word says that 'if your brother or sister sins, go and point out their fault, just between the two of you. If they listen to you, you have won them over. But if they will not listen, take one or two others along, so that every matter may be established by the testimony of two or three witnesses. If they still refuse to listen, tell it to the church; and if they refuse to listen even to the church, treat them as you would a pagan or a tax collector.'"

As my words settled, the virtual room became still. I could see the softening of my director's eyes as she recognized the scripture and understood exactly why I had called the meeting. Because despite all the things that seemed to separate us—race, color, and age—the Word of God united us. And from one woman of God to another, she could not deny the Truth that was spoken.

But the softening didn't last long. As her energy shifted to anger, she responded.

"I'm sorry, but I'm not going to sit here and listen to this drama!" the director exclaimed.

I could see the HR VP attempting to unmute herself to respond, but I beat her to it.

"Susan (name changed for confidentiality), I am a grown woman who is talking to another grown woman about their working relationship. I do not know what it is about me that triggers you, but I want to let you know here today, with an audience, that you cannot, will not, and may never again speak to me in the ways that you have. And moving forward, I hope that our interactions are more professional and pleasant with one another."

Again, the room was silent.

I'd done it. As David said to the Philistine, "you come against me with sword and spear and javelin, but I come against you in the name of the Lord Almighty, the God of the armies of Israel, whom you have defied." (1 Samuel 17:45) It felt darn good; like sunshine that warms you from the inside out. It felt like favor.

Moments later, I received an apology.

Down goes the giant.

In conquering my own personal giant, I realized this Truth: the Word of God exposes. While some attempt to hide behind its safety while excluding others, some of us use it to do as God intended. To shine light in a dark world.

ABOUT THE AUTHOR

NAYSHONDRA MERCER, MA, CPC, ELI-MP

Nayshondra Mercer, affectionately known as Coach Nay, is a Life and Leadership Transformation Coach, bestselling author, and Founder and CEO of Crossing Bridges Coaching & Consulting. She is known for helping changemaking women become what she calls "Untriggerable," leaders who refuse to be governed by old wounds, unmanaged triggers, or inherited narratives.

With more than a decade of experience in behavioral transformation, learning and development, and mental wellness advocacy, Nayshondra works at the intersection of healing and leadership. She challenges high-achieving women to stop performing resilience and start practicing emotional sovereignty. Her work centers on powerful boundaries, self-awareness, and leading from wisdom rather than survival.

Through her signature program, *I AM: Seeking Myself*, as well as her podcast and speaking engagements, she creates brave spaces where vulnerability becomes strength and hard conversations become catalysts for growth. Her message is clear: authenticity is not a branding strategy. It is a discipline.

Nayshondra is a contributing author to the #1 bestselling anthology *Awareness Put Me On*, where she shares her personal journey of faith and mental wellness. Whether coaching executives or facilitating dialogue, she is committed to helping women step fully into their voice, their authority, and their unapologetic truth.

PART III

CHOOSING THE HARD CONVERSATION

Candor, Accountability, and the Practice of Courageous Leadership

"Courage starts with showing up and letting ourselves be seen."

—Brené Brown

CHAPTER SIX

WHITNEY CARRINGTON

THE QUIET BUT ESSENTIAL WORK OF BRAVE LEADERSHIP

There are questions I ask myself every day. I remember the moment I first stepped into a leadership role. The offer letter came in and, with my heart racing, I rushed through what seemed to be the longest intro to see "We are pleased to extend you the job." I immediately started cycling through the typical emotions: ecstatic, nervous, a tinge of stress.

In the weeks leading up to my first day, a question kept lingering in my mind, and honestly, I still ask this question every day: "What kind of leader do I want to be?" I questioned if I was good enough. Would I be accepted? Did I truly belong in the room? Did I make the right decision? Am I ready? Did I just girl boss too far?! I recall calling mentors telling them I got the job, but asking whether I should take it. *I am comfortable where I am. What if this isn't a good decision?* I'd run through the list of excuses I had made up in my mind. But that is just it: I was comfortable where I was. I had set a goal to apply for this job and finally made it to my goal and as I started speaking truth to all of my inner thoughts I realized deep down the truth was…I *was* good enough. I trained and received the education necessary for this moment for years. I worked hard. I earned the opportunity.

I had served in leadership roles before in the community, in church, in my sorority, so what exactly made this any different? Nothing. You get up and put your pants on every day like everyone else, except now you get to wear a badge of honor knowing that the decisions you make could change the future of how others lead, change the trajectory of those you serve for the better, and have a larger impact on the world.

could change the future of how others lead, change the trajectory of those you serve for the better, and have a larger impact on the world.

It was very interesting to see how I was perceived by others. It was not an insult but insight. I recall once walking into a room and preparing a space for an inspection. I immediately unloaded my computer, water bottle, and two phones on the first empty space I could find. I was one of the first to arrive. Then others started trickling into the room, coming in and out. Contractors, maintenance, painters, plumbers—you name it. The space was a revolving door to make everything perfect for a passing score. I rolled up my sleeves, started grabbing boxes, and helped the staff unpack their materials, clean the surfaces, and sort through a "keep or discard" pile. After I left, I was tremendously pleased. I was so impressed by my interaction I sent an email to their supervisor telling them about my experience. I later found out that the supervisor immediately called the staff and asked, "Do you know who came to help you? Do you know who that was? Why didn't you tell me?" They merely thought I was a lady who worked in the building offering to help. That's exactly who I was and who I wanted and needed to be at that time.

On the complete opposite end, there have been times in my experience working I have settled on the edge of the room, intentionally not at the table, placing my materials down. Attendees start pouring in. I see familiar faces in a room chatting, planning an "offline" conversation after the meeting. The meeting begins, and everyone starts introductions. I introduce myself, rarely with my title, just my name and who I am supporting. I watch, take in the room, take in how I am perceived, who asks, "Well, do you have anything you'd like to contribute?" In some spaces I am big, I am bold, I ask questions, I challenge, but I always adapt to the room that I am in.

Why? Leadership is often immediately regarded as possessing a certain set of skills and strategy, speaking the language, using buzzwords and knowing all the acronyms,, or even how you physically present yourself—fresh manicured nails, heels, hair styled to perfection. It's less often regarded as the ebbs and flows of experiences shaped by an identity you were born into and the way the world sees you. For women from historically marginalized backgrounds, leadership frequently requires navigating spaces where voices are not always centered and leadership is perceived to be out of Black women's reach.

What I've learned is that leadership does not always reflect our assumptions and it rarely feels comfortable at first. To lead effectively, you must sometimes be willing to occupy multiple roles like being the administrator, being the person that is willing to clean, occupying the roles that were steppingstones to get to where you are now to listen, learn, absorb, and still move forward with clarity and personal conviction.

True leadership requires leaning into your strengths, acknowledging your weaknesses, embracing change even when it feels destabilizing, and not compromising your values. It requires courage to speak when silence feels safer, and resolve to act when avoidance is more comfortable.

LEADING THROUGH UNCERTAINTY AND FEAR

I started leading in my current role in March of 2020. To date, it's the bravest space that I have stepped into professionally. I started during the COVID-19 pandemic. Nothing I did at the time was part of what I interviewed for, but God prepared me for this moment. I was supporting public health response with no blueprint nor established relationships with information shifting at a rate that seemed faster than I could type an email. Work demanded immediate and around-the-clock action, clear judgment, and the ability to lead through rapidly changing public health guidance. While there were no standard operating procedures to fall back on nor transition plans to provide guidance, there was an urgent responsibility to protect the community I served. Avoiding hard conversations was not going to get me to where we needed to be. We had to keep the community safe and stick strictly to CDC and Public Health requirements early on so we could all be in our familiar spaces together again. The problems we faced in our area reflected what was happening on stages nationally: mask requirements, isolation, quarantine, social distancing (sorry, I don't mean to bring about PTSD.)

During this time, I had to create a brave safe space and step into rooms where fear, disagreement, and honesty could be named openly to enable better decisions in moments when avoidance felt even more tempting and comfortable behind a screen. Those spaces allowed us to act with urgency, equity, and accountability when the work demanded and depended on all three.

What became immediately clear was that avoidance of using my voice and discomfort with hard conversations were not an option. Delaying decisions or softening messaging to avoid tension did not make the situation safer. That made it more confusing. In the absence of clarity, fear can easily fill gaps. Because if you don’t make a decision, one will be made for you. Where you could have stood up, you might be sitting with the what-ifs of the voice you did not use.

I had to lead the building of systems in real time, where each component of my work required honest conversations about capacity, risk, and responsibility. Some decisions were unpopular. Many were uncomfortable. All of them were necessary.

So what does courage look like? For me, it is sticking to core values, setting boundaries, and taking accountability for only my mistakes and learning from them.

I often reflect on how I have been treated by those who have led me through my journey to leadership, and I try my best to make sure those I lead get my best self.

BRAVE SPACES AS AN EQUITY PRACTICE

Brave space is an equity practice because it changes *who is heard, how decisions are made, and whose needs are at the center of the work that is being done.* I recall sitting in a LeaderShape in college (see? I always had it in me), and we did a practice activity where they gave us a prompt and we were observed trying to conjure a solution to a problem. At the end we received feedback and they pointed out strengths and weaknesses for everyone. One of the pieces of feedback that stuck out most to me was how most were fighting to be heard and share their input. No one thought to ask the quiet people in the room; they often have the most valuable suggestions and solutions to the problems at hand.

In many professional spaces, expertise is not always received or perceived equally. For women and leaders from historically underrepresented backgrounds, credibility is often examined more closely, contributions are more readily questioned, and decisions are sometimes met with skepticism. This does not devalue WHO you are as a leader, but who THEY are in character. This reality continues to shape how leadership is experienced and exercised generationally.

Navigating these dynamics requires both clarity and restraint. There is often an unspoken pressure to over-prepare, over-explain, or soften one's expertise to be accepted. Living the familiar saying that you have to be "twice as good to be considered half as great" can be exhausting, particularly in environments where authority is measured by not just knowledge, but also perception. While these conditions can challenge confidence, you cannot allow any environment to compromise values, judgment, or integrity.

Over the years I have learned that credibility is not built through constant defense. Remaining grounded in evidence, policy, and purpose creates a steadiness that withstands doubt over time. Integrity becomes the anchor guiding my day-to-day decisions.

Upholding professional ethics and institutional responsibilities, and building community trust, requires separating personal praise from public service. Decisions must remain rooted in what is lawfully aligned with mission, not in reaction to bias or resistance. Find ways to color inside the lines differently.

Ultimately, I have learned that leadership is not validated by who affirms it in the moment, but by outcomes and the quality of the work, trust from the community, and sustainability of efforts. When leaders remain aligned with their values and beliefs, the weight of integrity will always outlast those who doubt us. That commitment to prioritize purpose over perception, though it can be hard at times, is what allows brave leadership to endure without compromise.

CARRYING THE LESSONS FORWARD: LEADERSHIP AS STEWARDSHIP

One of the most humbling and important responsibilities of leadership is deciding what *should not* be repeated. Over time, I have learned that brave leadership is not only about making difficult decisions in the moment, but also absorbing both positive and negative past experiences and using them to shape a healthier environment for those to come. Leadership is just a title; the most important piece is the integrity you put towards it and how you treat others.

Throughout my career, I have been lucky to have worked under many powerful female leaders who have modeled transparency, trust, and accountability. I have also worked in spaces where title and ranking are part of the foundational structure. Both experiences were formative, shaping the leader I am today. The positive examples showed me how courageous conversations can foster trust, even in high-pressure environments. The more challenging experiences taught me what happens when fear replaces communication, when expectations go unnamed, and when the pace of progress depends on the author.

As a leader, I am intentional and passionate about ensuring those who report to me or work alongside me get to experience a culmination of the positive experiences I have had each step of the way.

Protecting my team does not mean shielding them from difficulty; it means equipping them with context and clarity and building trust. I believe that leadership is a form of stewardship. When leaders take the time to reflect on their own experiences and name what they refuse to pass on, they can create environments where people can do hard work without unnecessary harm. That, to me, is the quiet but essential work of brave leadership.

Leadership is not perfect. Leading is not perfect. The work has constantly reminded me of my humanity. I learned from being willing to take accountability, from mistakes, and from…everyone. As a Black girl in a world full of bias, I once entertained the doubt that I even belonged in the room. Years past that whisper in my mind, what's echoed is the work itself affirming my belonging. I began this journey deciding what kind of leader I wanted to be. After a host of trials and seasons of learning under pressure, resilient is the leader I've become.

ABOUT THE AUTHOR

WHITNEY
CARRINGTON

Whitney Carrington is a public health practitioner in education with more than 15 years of experience advancing equitable access to care for students and families. She works at the intersection of health policy, school-based systems, and cross-agency collaboration, where decisions on paper must translate into real-life outcomes.

Whitney does not separate policy from people. She ensures policy protects those it is intended for.

Her career has spanned across hospitals, grassroots initiatives, local and federal agencies, and supporting communities from military families to children inside public school classrooms. She has strengthened school health infrastructure, led large-scale planning efforts, and guided teams through communicable disease response, substance use prevention, and COVID-19 recovery. Across every initiative, her focus remains the same: students should be safe, supported, and able to focus on learning.

Operating at the crux of policy, operations, and on-the-ground implementation, Whitney turns complex health regulations into practical systems schools can actually use. She builds sustainable health models that reduce barriers from the moment a student walks into a classroom.

At her core, Whitney believes schools are one of the most powerful access points for public health. When systems are thoughtful, relationships are strong, and communication is clear, health outcomes improve and families can trust that their children are protected while they learn.

CHAPTER SEVEN

ERNEST BONASERA

MY LEADERSHIP (AND MY LIFE) ROUGH DRAFTS

A few months ago, my wife sent me a clip of a podcast interview with Mel Robbins and Dr. Gabor Maté. It caused me to pause, reflect, and ultimately scrap and rewrite this entire chapter. In it, Dr. Maté shared an observation: when you're a parent of multiple kids, none of them are the same and none of them have the same parent. Your firstborn gets a version of you that's full of excitement, some anxiety, maybe some knowledge, and hopefully a plan. They're also getting someone who lacks any real experience. If you have multiple children, the younger ones get a parent who has (hopefully) learned from their mistakes, but might be in a different life situation. Their knowledge is different. Their skills are different. Their environment is different. The weight of their responsibilities – and their ability to lift that weight – is different. And the same applies for those in your care.

What hit me like a ton of bricks was that this message didn't only apply to parenting. It applied to all the titles we carry. For me, I'm a parent, a husband, a leader, a mentor, and if you are reading this now… I am officially an author too! Every single one of these titles has had different versions of me and has gone through different drafts – drafts I've personally gone through, but also drafts those in my care have had to experience. And those drafts are not final. They're just new and hopefully better versions of the ones before. And like parenting, leadership, and writing this chapter, the work is a series of crumpled-up sticky notes, and when done right, the opportunity to grab another notepad and try again.

What I can also tell you is that as I have grown and my titles have grown, the weight and responsibility has grown too, and this shit is heavy. It's one thing to carry your own goals and dreams, but once you start stacking on the goals and dreams of others, it becomes a new weight. You expect that over time it gets easier, but for me, it never has. What it has gotten is lighter. As you increase your skills, you gain tools and experience, and grow partnerships with people who can help. You don't eliminate the weight – you just make it easier to haul.

And there is no better way to build those muscles than by living in brave spaces and navigating bold conversations.

Here are a couple of mine…

LET'S TALK ABOUT SHITTY FIRST DRAFTS...

As a parent, my now 20-year-old got the early-20s version of me, living in an apartment with a fridge filled with WIC eggs and cheese. My future wife and I were doing our best to learn and follow all the rules while still learning about ourselves and each other. I mean, shit, I was still learning how to shave (as evident in all the pictures of me from that era where I rocked a pretty stupid-looking goatee)! We avoided screen time, read many books, earned a few stitches from falling drills not being put away properly (my bad), and we may or may not have had a close call with our kiddo and the consumption of cat poop (also my bad).

As a people leader, my first team got someone who was incredibly eager but lacked most of the important skills needed to lead and had virtually no experience. I was a top individual performer and showed enough potential for my boss to give me a shot at leadership. To that point, my only real leadership training was from how I'd been led in work, school, and sports, and maybe a few YouTube links I stumbled upon. And although I had a few good role models, most of my leadership examples were not people I wanted to be like. My inexperience showed itself pretty quickly in one of the most challenging conversations I'd ever had with my sales team.

I was a couple of months into leading and our team was underperforming toward our monthly goals. Remember, I was a top individual performer before I was promoted. Although I had my own ups and downs, I had never been on the bottom of a rank report, and as a new leader, I wasn't about to have my team show up there either. I also had a chip on my shoulder from being the leader of a satellite office. I felt like we had more to prove because all the other teams were in and around headquarters. They knew everyone by name, while our whole team was just lumped into being "Team Tucson." We had something to prove. After spending two hours on morning calls getting picked apart for our low numbers, I was pissed that we weren't already proving it.

I hung up the conference call. I remember pacing back and forth in my office for the next hour, trying to find the right words and the right energy to light a fire under my team. For some context: I had a group of incredible sales individuals. They had skill, had energy, knew how to make work fun, and most importantly (as I would find out soon enough), they truly cared about each other and the success of the team. I'd hired almost all of them myself and built trust with the others as a peer and someone they could depend on. When I stepped into that first leadership role, a big reason why was the support of my team. They'd vocalized that they wanted to be led by me. If it weren't for that support, I don't think we would have gotten through what came next.

I worked through a few ways I could share my frustration with the group and a couple ideas on how I could cascade belief. When all was said and done, I decided to hunker down into two emotions: anger and guilt! I stormed into our sales bullpen where they were all huddled and shouted out, "CONGRATULATIONS!"

That got their attention. I got a confused response.

"Congratulations?" they inquired, curious looks on their faces.

"Yeah. Congratulations!" I responded. "Your numbers all suck and now I can't pay my mortgage!"

Then I turned around and stormed right back out of the bullpen and into my office without saying another word.

I can imagine you're reading this and feeling the same way I am while writing and reliving it. Every time I think about that story, I cringe and shake my head. I can't even imagine what my team was feeling at that moment, but I can remember what they were saying – absolutely nothing. They were stunned by what came out of my mouth. So was I. I felt ashamed and disappointed in myself – I knew at that moment that I might have just lost the trust of these people I cared so much about. And what happened next didn't only change me as a leader; it changed me as a person.

After sitting there for a few minutes, I heard a knock on my office door. There was my team, looking both concerned for me and a little scared of what I might say next. They started by apologizing for underperforming and how they had let me and each other down. Then they shared what was getting in their way and they also shared what they believed I could and should do to help them get better. They also went on to share where they believed I'd fallen short on coaching and developing and where I lacked clarity in the goals and holding them accountable.

Because of the relationship we had as a team and their support of me as their leader, that unedited, unfiltered outburst of frustration gave them permission to be unfiltered too – and to do so in a better way than I had just minutes before. That was a messy-ass moment that taught me something foundational to everything I believe about leadership: honesty, even poorly delivered honesty, opens doors that politeness and silence keep closed.

I was so blessed to have a team that didn't shut down or get defensive. They met my raw and uncensored candor with their own. They heard my struggles, and that opened the door to tell me the truth about where they were struggling too. They could have just nodded, apologized, and gone back to their desks – that would have been the comfortable response. Instead, they created what I now recognize as a brave space by refusing to let my honesty be one-directional. They used this uncomfortable moment to bring the same vulnerability to me that I'd just dumped on them. And that moment of honesty changed how we functioned as a team, changed how I functioned as a leader, and showed me the risks of carrying all that leadership weight alone and the benefits of lifting it with others.

That moment taught me the power of messy honesty. But a few years later, I'd learn the opposite lesson: what happens when you stay silent in the moments that matter most.

ANOTHER ROUGH DRAFT AND THE COST OF STAYING QUIET

Fast forward another four or so years. I was still working through parenting rough drafts with my three kids. We were moving cities, changing schools, packing up houses – trying to keep everyone stable while they were all growing in all kinds of directions. At work, I'd moved from leading a sales team in southern Arizona to an area in northern Colorado, and had just accepted an opportunity to lead a sales organization covering the state of Washington. I was adding titles and responsibilities – shouldering more weight than I was capable of lifting on my own.

Within the first couple months of stepping into my new role, I was told that one of my new responsibilities as a director was to restructure our sales team and sales model. This included impacting the jobs of almost 200 people and asking them to reapply for roles that were drastically different from what they'd done in the past. Mind you, I was new to the region, new to my team, and new to the role of a director, and all the training and books I had read didn't cover that!

I received this news a few months before the organizational transition was set to happen. In those months leading up to it, I had several meetings with my peer team to talk through the changes that were coming, the risks, and how to best get our team through. I was overwhelmed and underskilled. I didn't know how to ask for help, or who to ask. I was still thinking like an area manager, like someone impacted by the change, not someone responsible for lessening the impact.

This was a massive decision that was going to impact more than 200 people – people I'd just started to get to know and was just beginning to build trust with. I'd come into the region selling vision and hope, helping them navigate the uncertainty that comes with getting a new leader, only to now be the one who would topple their world.

I just couldn't comfortably and compliantly move through a change like this without pushing back on what I wasn't ready to own.

I spent the next two months arguing the changes and trying to persuade my leadership to shift their decisions in rooms that were designed to make sure we had a voice but I now know were never designed to give us a vote. I'm sure my division leader still has nightmares about my 6:00 a.m. instant messages where I wanted to give him another reason not to move forward with this plan and my 8:00 p.m. calls trying to convince him there was another way. But I was having nightmares too — of this rollout going terribly wrong and us losing everyone on the team, our region never recovering, and me losing my job.

In the end, all that pushback and arguing did was take time away from the conversations I should have been having and the trust-building with my team that I'd need to push through what was about to come.

About 45 days before the change was set to go live, I brought my reporting managers into the fold. This was my leader of leaders team that would be tasked with helping me roll out these large-scale changes. Because I spent my first 45 days fighting the changes and not doing a great job of understanding them, my direct leaders spent the next 40 days having the same fights with me.

Even worse, I never got the chance to get myself comfortable with the change. I never got myself aligned, so I wasn't remotely prepared to help others get through it either. I now know why they say to put the oxygen mask on yourself first in emergencies.

When I finally was able to meet with my leaders, they gave me new reasons why they believed the change wouldn't work and new ideas that we might have wanted to consider instead. They presented risks I hadn't thought of and new challenges I hadn't considered. My head was still spinning, and my hope of making it through was dwindling. I would take all these bullet points to my executive and cross a few fingers and toes, hoping the company would hear our plight and magically decide not to move forward with the change.

Well, we all know how that story ends. The reality was that the company had locked in this decision long ago and there was no budging on moving forward with the changes. I know now that they brought us directors in to help support those changes and to see a preview months before it happened. I also know now that when I was allowed to bring my team in, my job wasn't to sit on the same side of the table and join them in battle – it was to sit at the head of the table and guide them through it.

I'd walk into meetings with my direct leaders, and I knew there were questions they weren't asking me. Just like I knew there were answers I wasn't giving them, some I didn't have and some I just didn't like. I was so focused on what I thought the company should do differently that I forgot to help my team understand what they should do next. I was having the conversation I wanted instead of the conversation they needed to hear. Where I was loud with my complaints to my direct leadership, I was quiet with my direction and intention for the team. I gave them space to voice their concerns, but didn't give them clarity on what they should truly be concerned about.

And just like the lesson I learned from that mortifying moment, but somehow forgot, honesty always opens doors. I was being honest in the wrong direction. I was pouring all my candor upward to leadership who'd already made their decision while staying carefully silent with the team who actually needed to hear from me. They needed honesty. They needed clarity. Because I wasn't being honest with myself and willing to accept the reality of what was going to change, I made things harder on myself and all those in my care.

It was five days before the change was officially implemented that we realized nothing was going to budge. I remember sitting with my direct leaders and having an "Oh shit!" moment about what was about to come. Not only did we have a short runway to get this communication out to our teams, but we also had an even shorter runway to get ourselves bought in and prepared to lead our teams through one of the most significant changes of their careers.

The change proceeded as planned. We lost almost 70% of our workforce and we spent the next 18 months rebuilding our teams and redefining our culture. And although we came out on the other side as the number-one sales team in the country (and did a whole bunch of other cool stuff along the way), I can't help but wonder what would have happened if I had been louder about a few things with my direct leaders.

What if I had focused less on what was changing that we could not control, and more on how I was truly feeling, how my team was feeling, how their people might end up feeling, and what actionable items we could take toward that? What would have been different if we could have spent 85 of the 90 days pushing a plan to mitigate risk and speed up the success of the transition, versus pushing back on a plan? What if, instead of five days to come to terms with the shift and scrambling to build a change-management plan in the final hours, we'd used 45 days as a leadership team to strategize on how to care for our people and the business?

How many people would have stayed during the transition? How much quicker could we have achieved success? How much stress and anxiety could we have prevented if I'd been more willing to have the harder conversation with the team, versus trying to prevent the hard conversations from happening?

The weight of that experience was crushing, impacting 200 people's livelihoods. I felt like I'd lost my team's trust and maybe, worst of all, my own belief in my abilities as a leader.

But I now know what would have made it lighter: stopping the shame of carrying it alone, bringing my direct leaders in earlier, and talking about the challenge we were up against, what we could do to help our people get through the change, versus fighting against it.

And I also know what grew out of it, even if it wasn't perfect. As a team, we built new tools for change management to make sure we didn't go through the same impact again. We created partnerships based on what we'd survived together instead of what we'd avoided. We built trust in each other, in our processes. I built trust in myself and the power of speaking up versus staying quiet in the most important spaces.

And I now know the weight doesn't disappear. I still think about that 70% regularly, but I now know how to turn failure into shared wisdom, and how to let others help me carry what I couldn't lift by myself.

Here's what I learned from that draft of leadership: there was no way my teams and I were going to agree with everything when it came to change. Good teams rarely do. But the great ones? They build the skills of navigating disagreements, getting the hard things out, and moving quickly to alignment. They make space for hard conversations, but they also make space for what comes after – and all the drafts they know will follow.

REMEMBER THAT THE ROUGH DRAFTS ARE THE WORK

I want to leave you with this. Just like your children never get the same parent, your teams never get the same leader. And that's not a flaw. It's evidence of growth. The people in your care change. You change. Your circumstances change. If everything feels the same year after year, that's usually a sign that nothing is stretching you and that you aren't growing.

And remember: leadership (and parenting too) never gets easier, but it does get lighter.

It gets lighter because you learn how to carry it. You build the skill of knowing which conversations to have and when – not storming into bullpens, but not staying silent for 85 days either. You add tools like change-management frameworks that you wish you'd had earlier. You gain experience that helps you recognize when you're fighting in the wrong room. And you stop trying to carry it all alone. You let your team knock on your office door, you bring your leaders in before day 86, you turn failures into shared wisdom instead of private shame.

So here's my invitation.

Write the shitty rough drafts. Be willing to say things imperfectly. Have the conversation when you need to, even if that's before you feel ready. Pick being honest over being comfortable. Your first draft of leadership, candor, or parenting doesn't have to be good. It just has to be honest. Because the alternative isn't that the hard conversations go away; it's that they come later, they feel heavier, and they are often lonelier. And by then, the people who needed to be part of them may no longer be there.

The work isn't avoiding the mess.

The work is in showing up again and again and being willing to write a better draft.

ABOUT THE AUTHOR

ERNEST BONASERA

Ernest Bonasera helps organizations close the gap between bold vision and the lived experience of their people. With nearly 20 years of leadership experience across hospitality, finance, telecommunications, and renewable energy, he specializes in transformational leadership development, employee engagement strategies, and building workplace cultures where people feel genuinely valued.

Ernest has partnered with teams to transform underperforming organizations into market leaders. He has supported complex merger and acquisition integrations, collaborated on profitable compensation structures, and facilitated leadership development programs that helped teams grow and thrive. Under his guidance, teams have earned national recognition and maintained best-in-class engagement scores.

As the founder of Defining What's Next (DWN) Consulting LLC, Ernest leads with a challenge-and-encourage approach. He believes people rise when they are seen clearly and supported honestly. Through executive coaching and team facilitation, he creates meaningful conversations that move organizations from extracting value from employees to building value with them.

Ernest holds a Bachelor of Science in Marketing and Consumer Behavior from Grand Canyon University and is a Prosci ADKAR & Change Management Practitioner. He served as Board Co-Lead for Junior Achievement of Washington. Ernest has also helped form, lead, and champion the corporate employee resource group Unidos and helped to grow Comcast's DEI initiatives.

Outside of consulting, Ernest enjoys spending time with his amazing wife, three beautiful kids, and two energetic dogs. When Ernest isn't impacting people and production you will often find him exploring the outdoors in the amazing Pacific Northwest.

PART IV

LEADING WITHOUT ARMOR

Presence, Vulnerability, and the Future of Authentic Leadership

"The work of the leader is to create conditions where the truth can be told."

—Parker J. Palmer

CHAPTER EIGHT

ANGELA DIXON WILLIAMS

MOVING FROM BLUEPRINT TO LEGACY

An ambulance ride, on a beautiful sunny day, was more than a physical disruption—it was the clearest signal that my life was no longer aligned.

Mornings are my favorite part of the day—the early hours when you wake up to the birds chirping and the sun rising.

That's how the day started on October 31, 2020.

It was a Saturday morning, finally a break from a week that felt like it would never end. I had spent long stretches of time glued to my office chair. Each day blurred into the next as I stared at my laptop. I hadn't stepped outside all week.

It was time to get up.

I had skipped all three of my weekly gym sessions and had promised myself I would make them up that weekend. *You'll feel better after the workout*, I told myself as I got dressed.

Heading down the hallway to check my email, I looked forward to getting out of the house and feeling that jolt of energy after a good workout.

But my legs felt unusually heavy that morning. My stride quickly turned into a slow shuffle. The muscles in my back started to contract, sending sharp bursts of pain down my legs.

Grabbing the front of my desk, I crouched to my knees. Slowly I slid to the floor landing on my side. I thought if I could just lie flat on my back, the pressure and the spasms would subside.

But each attempt to move intensified the pain.

The tears started to flow as I realized I was stuck.

I called for help.

As the sunlight streamed through the window the tears continued to fall. The room filled with fear. *What is this? Why can't I get off this floor?*

When the EMTs arrived, they rolled me onto the stretcher and carried me downstairs. I looked up at the beautiful blue sky as they eased me into the back of the ambulance.

My thoughts spiraled.

COVID was ramping up, and the hospital was the last place I wanted to be.

The doctors ran every test possible.

Nothing was broken. Stress was the culprit. Overworking. Lack of sleep. It had finally caught up with me.

The doctors and nurses were adamant about me leaving the hospital that day. The floor was filling quickly with COVID patients and that put me and my family at risk of exposure.

After hours of tests and a cocktail of pain meds, I was able to walk well enough to be released. I rested on Sunday and went back to work on Monday.

For the next several weeks the spasms would bring me to tears. Enduring the morning pain was the worst. To ease the pain I would walk, stand, sit—searching for a comfortable position until the medications finally kicked in, and then I started my workday.

Physical therapy was delayed. It aggravated the pain—a reminder that my body still needed time to recover.

"*Not everything that is faced can be changed, but nothing can be changed until it is faced.*" ***James Baldwin***

SEEING THE CRACK IN THE CIRCLE

Facing the Change Instead of Fixing It

Change doesn't always mean something is broken. Sometimes, it's what sits you down, commands your attention and points you toward something new.

A friend once told me that you reinvent yourself three to five times in your lifetime. At this highly seasoned Gen X phase, I found myself swimming in an ocean of change. *How do you lead through all of this?* I was waist-deep in figuring out life again—and so was almost everyone I knew. I could see it on people's faces and hear it in their voices, and even more clearly in their actions. The phrase "It's all too much" surfaced repeatedly in conversations. It was more than a sound bite—it was a shared expression of fatigue.

Conversation confirmed a collective sentiment: people were tired of doing more with dwindling resources. Executives and leaders across organizations were asking the same questions: *What are we doing? Who are we becoming?*

The crisis of burnout was on everyone's tongue. I watched them either avoid it, get rid of it, or wade through it. I was left asking myself, *What's next?*

My nervous system had been hijacked far too frequently by life's normal transitions. For some of us, midlife is a cluster of change—loss of family members and friends, caretaking responsibilities, career shifts, divorce and menopause. As the waves rolled in, grief needed to be redressed, relationships renegotiated and work life recalibrated. Meanwhile, my body was responding to "the change," reconstructing itself without my permission.

But these natural transitions didn't feel natural at all. The reality of normal had shifted. The world was different. And I was still becoming.

Looking back on that clear October morning, the ambulance ride was more than a medical emergency. The pain that day seemed abrupt, but the truth is I hadn't paid attention. The subtle signals had been there for a while. Even through the aftermath of discomfort, I kept on going—immersing myself in the daily routine of work. I sat in meetings discussing strategy while quietly navigating relationship endings and shifting family dynamics. My thought at the time was, *I've navigated these spaces and relationships this long; maybe staying in them wouldn't be so bad.* I was aware of the complexities of changing, and actively avoiding the pause required to understand it.

As a card-carrying member of the helper/fixer club, my library of self-help books is proof of my instinct to problem-solve. Certificates and degrees tucked away in boxes are the tell-tale signs of my appetite for expansion and the next opportunities to pivot. My natural inclination has always been to lean into those familiar patterns of righting the ship—if one thing doesn't work, try something else.

I can fix it.

But reinvention without deeper understanding seemed too shallow for this deeper life shift.

My inner thoughts began unraveling the roles wrapped up in beliefs and labels stitched into my identity. The weight of fixing was as heavy as the tension in my body the day of the ambulance ride.

Overriding the urge to overfunction and rebuild was the hardest part.

It was the moment I knew that things no longer fit.

I called this the *"Crack in the Circle™"*: the timely and untimely disruption that demands reflection on beliefs, relationships, and identities that once felt like enduring truths but no longer align with the life we are living.

Instead of fixing, I chose to make space for internal dialogue. What began with morning walks and reflective thoughts soon turned into journal entries, and eventually poetry. Over time, it became a calm and steady rhythm of self-inquiry—one that led me to ask deeper questions:

1. What is this change revealing?
2. Who is it about?
3. What does it require of me?
4. How do I want to respond, in alignment with who I am becoming?

BEGINNING WITH AWARENESS...
Continuing the Work of Becoming

My reflection takes me back to the end of 2023, a milestone of almost four years of study.

Experiential learning opened my eyes to how personal awareness, emotional patterns, and lived experience shape change and transformation within people and organizations.

Through my research, I was fortunate to speak with leaders across the country in different industries. These individuals shared their experiences with deep openness and vulnerability.

We discussed history, perceptions, and social factors that shaped the workplace. They were keenly aware of the conditions in organizations—the fractures in the cultures, structures, and morale. They saw the outdated systems and misaligned authority.

These leaders were deeply intuitive. They painted a vivid picture of the present while also imagining what the future might hold. Despite daily constraints, they spoke proudly of their contributions, successes, and their missions to make a difference.

It was their personal stories of self-leadership that stayed with me. I heard candid reflections that traced their leadership evolution across personal, professional, and communal intersections. For them, leadership wasn't a title—it was a lived practice embodied in how they showed up and the legacy they hoped to leave behind.

The connection between awareness, wisdom, and empathy (A.W. E.™) and the vulnerability that existed in their leadership highlighted a capacity gap present for me earlier in my career.

This experience sparked my desire to share my own leadership story. But if we're being honest, brave spaces to have bold conversations are rare—almost extinct. I had been quietly holding onto my own leadership lessons because I believed people gravitated more toward polished success stories instead of the gritty realities encountered along the way.

In 2024, my aspirations to have deeper leadership conversations were realized through an unexpected opportunity to do just that. Although hesitant at first, I joined a group of extraordinary leaders as a contributing author featured in *Awareness Put Me On.* These authors worked in industries across the country. Most of us were strangers—only a few of us had previously met. Our connection was simple: a willingness to write about a pivotal moment of awareness—the moment that expanded our capacity to lead.

There was no gatekeeping. No sugarcoating. We were responding to the call to deliver real-life lessons—the ones that often go unspoken.

From cover to cover, the book was authentic. The stories were a rearview mirror of lived experiences, wisdom earned, and insights shared with empathy. Both writers and readers were invited to step into the practice of conscious leadership.

My chapter, "The Blueprint of Authentic Leadership," intentionally wove together personal and professional experiences. Parts of my history revealed themselves, offering insights extending beyond models and frameworks.

There was a cadence to self-leadership in concert with conscious leadership—a rhythm that aligned with how one leads oneself and how one shows up inside communities and organizations.

The truth is that becoming never stops. Assigning a label to it might narrow possibilities still waiting to emerge.

It was this realization that led to a deeper question: What does leadership look and feel like when awareness and integration are fully aligned?

INTEGRATING THE LEADER WITHIN

Practicing Toward Legacy

That Crack in the Circle where things no longer fit was a reckoning to move beyond my awareness of this connection. For me, midlife was marked by unfolding family dynamics, divorces, and career change. My personal chaos wasn't much different from what I observed in organizations. Though the narrative was not precisely replicated, the experience felt the same.

Awareness alone is not enough. Without integration, it can leave us stuck—circling the same cycles. I had observed and studied informally and formally how leadership naturally takes form—exploring the thin line between self-leadership and organizational leadership. The pattern I was seeing in myself, and in the organization, was the urgency to resolve our discomfort.

WHAT HAPPENS WHEN YOU DON'T FIX IT

There were certainly days when I wanted to start over completely—build a new life from the ground up. At times, I believed I could fix everything, but that instinct would have ushered me back to the same predictable ending—the very thing that fueled my habit of fixing. It was the precursor to burnout.

Unlearning the urge to push forward without discernment and creating the space for integration were harder than I imagined.

Not fixing was unfamiliar. But it didn't cause things to collapse. Resolutions were not immediate, and uncertainty still lingered. Relationships were not magically mended, conversations were not easier, and the next endeavor was far from clear.

Yet the tension of urgency loosened its grip, making space where pressure used to live. Reactions slowed and observation opened.
The paradox of discomfort is that the faster we try to solve it, the less we allow it to shape us. And without that shaping, we cannot adapt—we only react.

I was noticing how often my instinct to fix was less about solving a problem and more about relieving the discomfort of not knowing. When I allowed the discomfort to stay, it began to teach. The lessons sharpened my awareness of patterns I had previously sprinted past.

In pausing, I realized that leadership—whether in organizations or in life—is not always about restoring order quickly. Sometimes it is about allowing disruption to reveal what no longer fits.

That realization changed how I approached both my personal life and my work. The same discipline I used with organizations—creating space for clarity, trust, and discernment—was now being practiced inwardly.

And the lesson was unmistakable: when we stop fixing, we start seeing.

My leadership work in organizations had mostly centered on restoring clarity and trust, when the things that once worked no longer fit. This is the point when capacity expands—for deeper listening, wiser discernment, and choosing response over reaction. It wasn't a fast fix or a surface reinvention. It required a shift in mindset—cultivating the clarity, composure, and consistency to coexist with change. I asked myself, *What would happen if I turned this practice inward?* I paused the autopilot to reflect on what was next …

Because two things can be true: a disruption can require reinvention and demand refinement. The discipline is knowing which is which—and having the composure to pause long enough to discern the difference.

Integration was the test—the daily practice of refinement and the consistency required to move people and organizations with change rather than against it. I had decided to take a page out of my own book, sit with the change, and create space to gain clarity, self-trust, discernment, and confidence.

THE PRESENCE OF AN INTEGRATED LEADER

Clarity, Composure, Consistency

As leaders, we can create our own spaces for meaningful conversation about leadership. As I reflected on my experiences, I noticed that leadership presence could be understood through three essential capacities: Clarity, Composure, and Consistency. These insights have evolved into a simple reflection that I've used to understand how my leadership presence is experienced by others.

The Integrated Leader™ is who you become when you don't retreat. It is what leadership looks like when Clarity, Consistency, and Composure are present. It reflects the alignment of mind, body, and purpose in leadership—shaping how you experience yourself and how others experience you.

The Growth Space™ 5-Question Leadership Reflection is a structured check-in that reveals how people you've worked with perceive your leadership presence. It collects the impact you've had on colleagues and collaborators.

The reflection is not about praise or critique. It is an inquiry into presence—the way people feel, think, and function around you. In many cases, others perceive the small cracks in our leadership patterns long before we recognize them ourselves.

I invite you to try it and share it with trusted colleagues and collaborators who are willing to provide their insights. It's important to explain this is reflective feedback. Accolades and critiques have their place, but this goes deeper.
At first, it may feel unfamiliar to both give and receive this kind of reflection. But over time, it creates the kind of awareness that strengthens leadership from the inside out.

Leadership is often evaluated by results, titles, or authority. This reflection focuses on something deeper—leadership presence. During my reflections, it was leadership presence and impact that sparked my curiosity. These five questions invite colleagues and collaborators to reflect on how your leadership influences clarity, emotional stability, trust, and thinking in the environments you help shape.

1. When you think about working with me, how did you feel about how decisions were made and conversations were held?
2. In moments of tension or uncertainty, how did my presence affect the room—if at all?
3. What pattern did you notice in how I showed up over time?
4. Did working with me help you trust yourself or think more expansively?
5. If you were describing my leadership style to someone else—without using titles or roles—what would you say?

These questions uncover something often overlooked in traditional leadership assessment. When the details of the last problem you solved are a distant memory, the presence of the integrated leader is what people will remember. They remember how they felt sitting next to you and how you drew their voices into the room. They remember whether your presence remained calm and steady under pressure, putting others at ease. And they remember whether you created space for their confidence to narrow or expand. These are the unforgettable impressions that form your reputation of clarity, composure, and consistency. This is the kind of quiet influence that turns leadership into legacy.

ARCHITECTING THE LEGACY

The integrated leader leads from a grounded presence. At this intersection—where personal awareness, emotional patterns, and lived experience quietly shape how we develop our personal and professional operating models—we are confronted with a crucial question: *How do we coexist with change?*

This prompts me to think more deeply on what leadership means in this context. I find myself grappling with challenging questions about who I am becoming as I continue to learn and grow. For me, this journey has meant understanding how leadership shows up not only in organizations, but also in my personal life.

I am someone who experiments with authority and integrations—designing environments that help people break the cycle of overfunctioning in broken systems and avoid burnout and build sustainable growth. Most of my work focuses on helping leaders regain clarity and self-trust when what used to work no longer fits. From there, we create space for integration.

Transformation begins the work. Integration does the job. Legacy is the quiet result.

The real legacy we leave is not in titles we hold or the systems we build, but in the courage to share the lessons of who we are becoming—the work that becoming asks of us.

ABOUT THE AUTHOR

ANGELA
DIXON WILLIAMS

Angela Dixon Williams is a leader in leadership and organizational development who believes meaningful change begins with awareness and the courage to lead with intention. With more than 20 years of experience supporting programs across federal and non-profit sectors, her work spans program management, organizational development, cultural intelligence, diversity and inclusion, and change management.

Angela is known for helping organizations navigate complexity while keeping people at the center of the work. She has led initiatives ranging from policy and technology implementation to large-scale program expansion, bringing together diverse teams to solve problems, exchange ideas, and build stronger, more connected workplaces. Her approach focuses on helping organizations understand their culture, strengthen relationships, and create environments that empower people to grow. Angela holds a master's degree in Organization Development from Pepperdine University and a bachelor's degree in Business Administration from the University of Maryland. She also holds certifications in Diversity, Equity, and Inclusion from Georgetown University, as well as credentials in Change Management, Leadership Coaching, Human Resources, and Program Management.

She is also a bestselling contributing author of the anthology Awareness Put Me On. Angela is a thoughtful writer who explores the intersection of leadership, lived experience, and personal becoming, often weaving poetry into her insights on self-leadership and growth. She believes leadership rooted in awareness, reflection, and intentional action creates space for transformation—both within organizations and within the people who lead them.

Shared Growth is the Leadership Legacy.

CHAPTER NINE

BRANDON T. JONES

PRESENCE IS THE NEW POWER

I used to believe leadership was about having the answers; the strategy, the plan, the five-year roadmap that made the board nod and the team feel steady.

Then cancer took every single one of mine away.

There is no MBA class for the moment your oncologist says "stage four." The room was too quiet. I remember the hum of the fluorescent lights and the faint smell of antiseptic. The doctor's lips kept moving, but the word *four* echoed louder than everything else. My hands were resting on my knees, perfectly still, as if my body understood something my mind had not yet caught up to; that the life I had carefully planned had just split in two. There is no executive coaching framework for the day your calendar, once color-coded and optimized, shrinks to infusion appointments and scans. There is no leadership retreat that prepares you for the silence of 3:17 a.m., when your body is exhausted, but your mind is bargaining with God.

In that season, I lost more than health. I lost my titles: CEO, CIO, board member, strategic advisor. Those words had weight. They organized rooms. They gave me a place to stand.

But when you're lying in a hospital bed, stripped of your calendar and your competence, titles dissolve. They cannot hold you. They cannot comfort your children. They cannot answer the question that begins whispering in the dark: *Who are you when you are no longer useful?*

That question is where my leadership began again.

PERFORMATIVE LEADERSHIP

Before cancer, I would've told you I was a present leader. I was visible, engaged, decisive. I ran meetings with crisp agendas and left with clear next steps. My teams delivered. My organizations grew. I was busy in all the ways our culture applauds.

But cancer has a ruthless way of exposing what is real and what is rehearsed.

During recovery, I began to see something uncomfortable: much of what we call leadership today is performance, not in the theatrical sense, but in the protective one.

We show up as we think leaders should. We speak in tones that signal authority. We nod at the right moments. We say, "Great conversation!" when nothing has actually shifted. We perform busyness. We perform alignment. We perform confidence.

And underneath it all, we are often afraid.

Afraid to say the thing that might disrupt harmony. Afraid to admit we do not know. Afraid to slow down in a world addicted to motion.

I remember one boardroom before my diagnosis. Ninety minutes into a meeting, slides had been presented, opinions aired, and polite agreement exchanged. We were exhausted and somehow nowhere.

Finally, I asked, "What decision are we actually making today?"
Silence.

Not disagreement. Silence.

We had been performing momentum. We had not been leading.

At the time, I saw it as a tactical miss. In hindsight, it was a spiritual one.

Leadership that is not anchored in identity will always drift into performance. And performance cannot sustain you when your life is on the line.

WHEN MORTALITY INTERRUPTS YOUR RESUME

After my Whipple surgery and thirty-seven rounds of immunotherapy, my body felt like a foreign country. There were days I couldn't stand without bracing myself. Days when fatigue pressed so heavily on my chest that even conversation felt like labor.

In that state, I could not perform. I did not have the energy to impress anyone. I did not have the stamina to maintain the image of the unshakeable executive. I had to choose where to spend my limited strength.

That is when a new question replaced all the old ones: *How present can I be today?*

Not: *How much can I produce?*
Not: *How much can I prove?*
But: *How fully can I show up?*

Presence, I discovered, is not passive. It is powerful.

Presence means you are not editing yourself for comfort. Presence means you are not scanning the room to calibrate your truth. Presence means you are willing to feel what is actually happening, in you and around you.

In that season, my children did not care about my quarterly performance. They cared whether I was there. Whether I could look them in the eye. Whether I could tell them the truth without hiding behind optimism.

My team did not need a superhero CEO. They needed a human one. They needed to know I was not pretending. That I was not minimizing the gravity of the moment. That I trusted them enough to be honest.

And I realized something I had missed in all my years of achievement: you cannot lead from labels. You can only lead from identity.

CLARITY: SAYING WHAT IS ACTUALLY TRUE

The first pillar that emerged from that season was clarity.

Clarity is not about having all the answers. It is about naming the real question.

In organizations, confusion is often tolerated because conflict feels dangerous. We move forward with half-formed assumptions, hoping alignment will emerge through momentum. It rarely does.

Clarity requires courage because it demands that someone say, "We are avoiding the real issue."

I began to practice two questions in every meeting: *What decision are we making today? What happens if we do nothing?*

These questions seem simple. They are not. They cut through performance. They expose ambiguity. They reveal when we are hiding behind busyness.

In my personal life, clarity meant saying to my wife, "I am scared." Not, "I am fine." Not, "We will get through this." Just the truth.

Clarity invites connection. Performance protects distance.

When leaders choose clarity, they create brave spaces—rooms where the unspoken can be spoken without punishment, where dissent is not disloyalty, where honesty is not career suicide.

But clarity alone is not enough.

RHYTHM: DESIGNING THE CADENCE OF TRUST

Before cancer, my calendar was a badge of honor. Back-to-back meetings. Travel. Speaking engagements. Strategy sessions. I equated density with importance.

Illness dismantled that illusion.

When your body enforces rest, you begin to see the frantic pace for what it is: noise.

Organizations have rhythms whether we design them or not. Most are reactive. Meetings recur because they always have. Conversations spiral because there is no intentional structure. Teams drift because there is no cadence of reflection.

I began asking different questions about recurring meetings: *Why does this exist? What changes because we met?*

If the answer was nothing, we redesigned it—or we eliminated it.

Rhythm is the architecture of alignment. It is the steady drumbeat that keeps people from burning out or checking out.

In my own recovery, rhythm looked like something far less glamorous: short walks, measured conversations, and a deliberate return to work instead of a dramatic re-entry.

I could not sprint. I could only sustain.

And sustainable leadership is far more powerful than sporadic intensity.

Brave spaces are not created in one explosive moment. They are cultivated through consistent, intentional rhythm. Through meetings where candor is normalized. Through leaders who return, again and again, to the real questions.

COURAGE: THE CONVERSATION YOU ARE AVOIDING

If clarity is naming truth and rhythm is designing alignment, courage is acting anyway. Courage is not bravado. It is the quiet willingness to risk misunderstanding for the sake of integrity.

During treatment, I realized something deeply uncomfortable: I had built a life where I was indispensable.

That felt like leadership. It felt powerful.

But underneath it was fear.

Fear that if I was not central, I was not valuable. Fear that if I stepped back, everything would collapse. Fear that my identity was inseparable from my output.

Cancer forced me to relinquish control. To trust my team. To allow others to lead.

And in doing so, I confronted a harder truth: some of my indispensability was ego.

Courage required me to say, "You can handle this." Courage required me to step out of meetings and let others speak. Courage required me to redefine my worth beyond performance.

In organizations, the most courageous question is often this: What is the cost of not acting?

We frame decisions around risk. But inaction has a cost too—a cost to culture, a cost to trust, a cost to momentum.

The conversation you are avoiding is often the one that will liberate your team.

The brave space is not created by comfort. It is created by someone willing to go first.

FROM TRANSPARENCY TO VULNERABILITY

There is a difference between transparency and vulnerability.

Transparency is sharing facts. Vulnerability is sharing impact.

I could tell you my diagnosis. That is transparency.

I could tell you how terrified I was to leave my children without a father and what it feels like to write each child a letter before surgery, in case I did not make it through. One night, after the house had gone quiet, I sat at the kitchen table with a yellow legal pad. The only light came from the small lamp over the sink. I could hear the refrigerator humming and the occasional creak of the house settling. My hand hovered above the page longer than it wrote. I wasn't drafting notes. I was trying to find the words my children might one day read if I wasn't there. That is vulnerability.

TRANSPARENCY INFORMS. VULNERABILITY CONNECTS.

In leadership, we often offer controlled transparency. We share updates, metrics, even setbacks. But we rarely invite people into the emotional house.

Vulnerability says, "This is hard." It says, "I do not have this figured out." It says, "I need you."

When I returned to work after treatment, people did not ask first about strategy. They asked, "Are you okay?" What they were really asking was, "Can we trust you again? Are you fully here?"

Trust is built when leaders are witnessed without armor.

In a conscious leadership culture, vulnerability is not weakness. It is a signal of strength. It tells people they do not have to pretend either.

Brave spaces are born when leaders stop editing themselves for comfort.

IDENTITY BEFORE PERFORMANCE

In the darkest nights of my illness, I had to answer the question I had spent years postponing: *If I am not my title, who am I?*

Not the CEO. Not the strategist. Not the award recipient. Who?

The answer emerged slowly, not in a lightning bolt but in a series of quiet realizations.

I am a husband. I am a father. I am the last surviving son of parents who have loved and supported me through every chapter of this journey. I am a man of faith. I am someone who believes in building things that outlast me. I am someone who wants to love well. I am someone who wants to create spaces where others thrive.

Leadership rooted in identity is different from leadership rooted in achievement.

Achievement-driven leadership asks, "*How do I win?*" Identity-driven leadership asks, "*Who am I becoming?*"

Achievement-driven leadership is fragile. It collapses when outcomes falter.

Identity-driven leadership is resilient. It persists when circumstances shift.

When you know who you are, you can walk into hard conversations without collapsing. You can say the unpopular thing. You can hold silence. You can let others shine.

Because your worth is not at stake. *Brave Spaces, Bold Conversations* is not a slogan. It is a discipline.

A brave space is not one where everyone feels comfortable. It is one where people feel safe enough to be real.
That kind of environment begins with leaders who are willing to be witnessed.

The psychology of performance tells us that when we know we are being watched, we tense. We brace. We perform.

But the most compelling leaders do something different. They allow themselves to be seen without resisting the gaze. They shift from self-consciousness to service, from *How am I coming across?* to *Are they receiving what they need?*

That shift changes everything.

When a leader stops performing, the room relaxes. Conversations deepen. People stop managing impressions and start telling the truth.

And that is where trust begins.

THE INVITATION
If you are reading this, you likely carry responsibility. Titles. Influence. Decisions that shape other people's lives.

I want to ask you the question cancer asked me: *If all your titles disappeared tomorrow, who would you be?*

And then:
Where are you performing instead of being present?

What meeting needs clarity instead of motion?
What rhythm needs redesign instead of endurance?
What conversation requires courage instead of avoidance?

Leadership today does not need louder voices. It needs clearer ones. Leaders who are willing to say, "This is what is true." Leaders who design cadence instead of chaos. Leaders who act not because it is safe, but because it is right.

Presence is the new power.
Not charisma. Not control. Not constant visibility.

Presence.

Because when you are fully present, people do not just follow your strategy. They trust your heart.

And in a world starving for authenticity, that may be the boldest conversation of all.

ABOUT THE AUTHOR

BRANDON T. JONES

Brandon T. Jones is the Founder and CEO of Javelin Digital, a strategic storytelling and visualization firm that helps senior leaders move from complexity to clarity in high-stakes environments. He served as CEO of Throughline, an enterprise design and strategy company partnering with over 150 organizations across the public and private sectors to translate intent into measurable impact.

A former two-time Chief Information Officer, Brandon has led technology and operations for organizations managing multi-million-dollar budgets and global teams. His experience spans defense, industrial base modernization, enterprise transformation, and digital strategy. Known for aligning boards, executives, and operators around a shared vision, he builds systems that drive execution, not just ideas.

At his core, Brandon is a translator of complexity. He believes clarity is not cosmetic. It's courageous. It requires naming what is true, aligning stakeholders around shared meaning, and moving forward with conviction. Brandon holds a B.A. in Computer Science from Saint Mary's College of Maryland and a Georgetown University executive certification in facilitation. His leadership has been recognized with the Washington Business Journal C-Suite Award and AFCEA's 40 Under 40 honor. He serves as Board Vice Chair of the Maryland Center on Economic Policy and as a board member of Perspective Equity Partners. He is also an active member of the Young Presidents' Organization (YPO).

A husband, father of three, and a cancer survivor, Brandon speaks openly about resilience, courage, and leading through adversity. He believes clarity, rhythm, and courage are the foundations of high performance in business and life.

CHAPTER TEN

B. MARIE ADAMS

CODE-SWITCHING TO CODE-CREATING: RECLAIM YOUR VOICE IN SPACES NOT BUILT FOR YOU

I learned early that how I showed up mattered—sometimes before I ever had the chance to show up at all. Even my name was part of that story. Before I was born, my parents made a decision founded in love, strategy, and protection. They chose a name that would give me the best possible chance within a world that hadn't yet decided how it would receive me.

Beth Marie Adams

It's a name that moves easily through spaces.
It doesn't raise questions.
It doesn't force assumptions.

And in the 1980s on Long Island, New York, it certainly wasn't a name most people expected to be attached to a young Black girl. But my parents' choice wasn't about erasing identity—it was about providing access. About opening doors before I ever had to knock. And in many ways, it worked. I moved through spaces where my résumé spoke before my background was questioned. Where I was granted entry into rooms that might have been harder to access otherwise. But access has a way of revealing truth.

I remember being seated in a waiting area for an interview, surrounded by other candidates. The room was nearly full—young people shifting in their seats, some reviewing notes, others quietly watching the door.

After about fifteen minutes, a sharply dressed, middle-aged white woman stepped out and called, **"Beth Adams."**

I raised my hand. "Here."

She looked down at the paper.
Then up at me.
Then back down again.

"Beth… Adams?" she repeated—this time, not as a call, but as a question.

"Yes," I said. "That's me."

She hesitated—just for a moment—but long enough.

Then she pulled herself together and said, "Right this way."

It was slight.
Quick.
Easy to dismiss if you weren't paying attention.

But I noticed.

Because that wasn't the first time my name had unlatched a door—only for my presence to make someone pause once I walked through it.

And it wouldn't be the last.

Over time, I came to understand something that no one teaches you—but many of us learn:

Access and acceptance are not the same thing.

Because once you're in the room, a different kind of navigation begins.

I learned early that how I showed up mattered just as much as what I knew—and that I would have to demonstrate that knowledge, consistently and repeatedly, to retain that access.

WHERE CODE-SWITCHING BEGINS

For me, code-switching didn't start in the workplace. It started at home. In my African American household—as in many others—presentation wasn't optional. It was taught. Modeled. Expected.

Sunday mornings were a lesson in it.

Our hair was pressed with hot combs or braided with bows on Saturday night. Clothes were laid out and ironed to a razor's edge. You put on your Sunday best. And when we arrived at church, we sat together—and don't you even think about acting out.

You carried yourself a certain way. You understood that how you presented yourself did not reflect just you—but your family.

Before visiting someone else's home, there were explicit instructions:

- Behave.
- Don't ask for food or drink.
- Every adult is to be greeted with Ms., Mr., Aunt, or Uncle—whether they were related to you or not.
- Don't touch anything that doesn't belong to you.
- Don't listen to adult conversations.

There was an understanding that you were representing more than yourself—you were representing your upbringing. Even something as small as a trip to the grocery store carried expectations. A look from my mother—just a look—was enough. No words needed. If my hand even reached toward something I hadn't been given permission to have, that look would send it right back to my side. Because I already knew. That was training.

At home, language mattered too. If I came home from school and started recounting my day using slang or jargon, my father would correct me.

Not harshly—but consistently.

He would make me repeat what I said—properly. Over and over again, until it was clear. Because in his mind—and in his experience growing up under Jim Crow laws in the South—how I spoke would shape how I was received. And how I was received would shape my opportunities. So before I ever stepped into a professional environment, I was already being prepared for it.

Prepared for how I needed to show up. How I needed to speak. How I needed to behave in spaces that might not automatically extend grace.

What I understand now is that it wasn't just parenting.

That was preparation. That was protection. That was a strategy.

I was always being prepared for how I had to enter the world—where second chances were rare for people like me, and stereotypes about who people believed I was had to be overcome before I was ever fully seen.

By the time I entered professional spaces, I wasn't learning how to code-switch—I was refining a vernacular I had been taught my entire life.

WHEN EXCELLENCE ISN'T ENOUGH

It didn't happen in one defining moment. It was a slow unfolding—a series of small wins, quiet observations, and uncomfortable realizations that, over time, became impossible to overlook. When I started new roles early in my career, I was intentional about how I showed up. I stayed quiet in meetings. I observed more than I spoke. I made sure I didn't come across as too eager, too assertive, or too much. I had already learned how quickly perception could shift.

So I did what I thought was right. I became the team player.

When I finished my work early, I asked how I could help others. I took on extra assignments. I volunteered for the tasks no one else wanted. I bent myself into a version of what I believed leadership expected—flexible, agreeable, dependable.

And I delivered.

Every time.

But over time, I started to notice something.

The recognition didn't come. The promotions didn't follow. The effort was there. The results were there.

But the outcomes didn't align.

And then one day, while sitting at lunch with another new hire, the disconnect became undeniable.

We were talking casually when he mentioned his salary.

I paused.

Then I calculated it (because I'm wired that way—I have a background in applied mathematics).

I was making **$0.76 for every $1 he made.**

Seventy-six cents. I sat with that number longer than I sat with the conversation. Because it didn't make sense.

I was a Magna Cum Laude graduate. I finished college in three years. I came from a prestigious Historically Black College and University.

I completed more tasks than anyone on the team.

And yet, I was earning significantly less than a colleague who:

- Barely graduated
- Got the job through a personal connection
- Took on fewer assignments

Something in me *shifted.* Not in a way that anyone in that room could see. But internally, something cracked open in me. Because at that moment, I realized:

Excellence alone was not enough.

CHOOSING MYSELF: FROM PROVING TO LEADING

For the first few years of my career as a software engineer, I became used to proving myself. Assignment after assignment. Project after project.

I often carried heavier workloads than my peers. I took on the most complex problems. The work others avoided—or weren't asked to do. I became known as "Ms. Fix-It" I was assigned the more disaster-prone projects, but I always turned them around.

I was frequently the only Black person in the room.

Often one of the very few women. Sometimes both. And still—I delivered. Despite microaggression and slick remarks. I proved "I belonged" with them. But somewhere along the way, I started asking a different question.

Not *"How do I prove myself?"*

But **"Why am I still trying to?"**

Because the truth was: I already knew what I was capable of. I had the receipts. Every completed project. Every solved problem. Every system that ran because of my work.

I wasn't just good at my job. I was excellent.

And once I accepted that—fully, without hesitation—everything began to shift. It took time, but I started speaking differently.

More directly. More confidently. Less concerned about how my voice would be received and more focused on what needed to be said. Because confidence grounded in evidence doesn't need to ask for permission. It asserts itself, and so did I. And then came one of the most important decisions of my career. I stopped waiting for someone else to recognize my value.

I chose myself and gave myself a promotion.

I left. And I stepped into a role that paid me $35,000 more. That decision wasn't just about compensation. It was recognition of my value. It was about alignment.

It was about refusing to stay in spaces that benefited from my excellence but hesitated to acknowledge it. And that shift didn't just change my career. It changed how I saw myself in every room I entered. I no longer questioned whether I deserved to be there. I started questioning whether the room deserved me.

SHOWING UP WITHOUT PERMISSION

That internal shift didn't stay internal.

It showed up—visibly, unapologetically—in how I entered every room.

For a long time, I had convinced myself there was a "right" way to look in corporate spaces.

Black suits.
Navy suits.
Neutral tones.
Structured. Safe. Controlled.

The corporate uniform. It wasn't assigned—but it was understood. And I followed it. Because I had learned that presentation could determine access. But as my confidence grew, so did my willingness to release the version of myself I had carefully constructed for acceptance.

And it didn't happen all at once. It started with small rebellions.

My earrings got bigger.
My lipstick got bolder.
My bracelets stacked higher—announcing my presence with every movement.

Then came the shoes.

Bright stilettos—blues, yellows, reds—colors that refused to shrink.

And then my hair.

I began to experiment.

Blonde.
Copper.
Red.

Each change was a step closer—not just to expression, but to truth. Because in Black culture, hair has never just been hair.

It is history. It is identity. It is communication.

It carries the legacy of a people whose beauty has been questioned, regulated, and redefined by others. From braids that once mapped escape routes during slavery, to styles that have been labeled "unprofessional" in modern workplaces, Black hair has always existed at the intersection of culture and control. For Black women especially, our hair is our crown. It reflects how we see ourselves—and often how the world sees us. And for generations, we've been taught—directly and indirectly—that in order to succeed, that crown had to be altered.

Pressed.
Straightened.
Tamed.
Hidden.

For some it's preference, but for others, it's conditioning. So when I made the decision—about fifteen years into my career—to do the "big chop"… it wasn't just a hairstyle change.

It was a release.

I stopped perming my hair.
Stopped wearing weaves.
And chose to wear it natural—curly, full, expansive.

Unapologetically mine.

And I won't pretend it was an easy decision. Lord knows some days I questioned my choices. After hours and hundreds of dollars on both styles and products, I found my look.

And something unexpected happened.

It wasn't my hair that took center stage.

It wasn't the earrings. Or the shoes. Or the color.

It was my presence.

My experience. My clarity. My leadership.

My ability to create space where others felt seen, heard, and valued.

I began to embolden others to speak up. To participate. To bring their full selves into the work. And people responded. They wanted to work with me. To learn from me. To grow within the environments I was helping create. I became a mentor—not just to women, but to anyone willing to learn. Because when you stop shrinking, you create space for others to expand. The impact extended beyond individual moments. The teams I led became known for their culture. The programs I built became sought after. When I posted positions, applications came in faster than we could process them.

Not because of a title, but because people wanted to be part of something that felt inclusive, empowering, and real. I received awards. Built communities. Created programs that outlasted my tenure. Helped develop the next generation of leaders. But even with all of that—there was one moment that meant more than anything else.

THE HALLWAY MOMENT

Twenty years into my career, serving as an Enterprise Architect and Branch Chief working within the US government, I was walking through the building on my way to a meeting.

My hair was out—an auburn-red natural afro, full and wide. I wore a floral outfit—blues and oranges—and heels that made their presence known with every step. Two young women I had never met stopped me in the hallway.

"Hi, are you Beth Adams?"

"Yes, I am."

They smiled—excited, a little nervous.

"We just wanted to tell you… we see you."

They told me how they would watch me walk through the halls.

How my outfits stood out.
How my natural hair inspired them.

And then they said something that stayed with me:

"When we found out you're a senior technical manager and architect—we were blown away.. There are so few of us in that type of position, but you're there and being your authentic self."

"You inspire so many of us."

"We started wearing our natural hair too. Keep doing what you're doing."

I thanked them and spoke with them briefly about their roles, and then continued on to my meeting. But that moment stayed with me.

Because what I realized in that moment was this: I wasn't just showing up as myself. I was giving others permission to do the same.

That impact—that quiet shift in someone else's confidence—meant more than any award I had received. More than any promotion I had earned. Because it wasn't about recognition. It was about **real** representation.

THE PEACE ON THE OTHER SIDE

What I found on the other side of code-switching wasn't just confidence.

It was peace. A peace that comes from no longer shapeshifting into who you think people want you to be. A peace rooted in alignment—between identity and expression, voice and presence. A peace that no performance could ever provide. Because authenticity doesn't just change how others see you.

It changes how you experience yourself.

And for the first time in a long time— I wasn't adjusting to the room. I was walking into it whole.

I started this journey with a name.

A name chosen with intention.
A name designed to open doors.
A name meant to give me a chance in spaces that might not have otherwise made room for me.

And it did. It gave me access. But access was never the destination. Because once I walked through those doors, I learned that entry is only the beginning.

What you do once you're inside—how you show up, how you speak, how you lead—that's where the real work begins. For a long time, I believed that success meant learning how to navigate the system.

Understanding the rules.
Reading the room.
Adjusting where necessary.

And to some extent, that was true. Those skills got me in the door. But they weren't enough to allow me to fully exist there. What I came to understand—through experience, through growth, through moments that challenged and reshaped me—is this:

I was never meant to spend my life translating myself for acceptance.

I was meant to lead in a way that made translation unnecessary.

That is the difference between code-switching and code-creating.

Code-switching helps you survive the system.

Code-creating allows you to transform it.

It's choosing to:

- Speak with clarity instead of caution
- Lead with authenticity instead of adaptation
- Create environments where others don't have to shrink to succeed

It's understanding that your presence—fully expressed—is not a liability. It's a catalyst.

When my parents named me, they gave me access. When they raised me, they gave me strategy. When I stepped into my career, I learned how to navigate. But when I chose to be fully myself—that's when everything changed. Because the greatest impact I've had hasn't come from fitting into spaces. It has come from expanding them. From building teams where people feel safe to contribute. From mentoring individuals who needed to see what was possible. From creating cultures that value not just performance—but presence. And from moments like the one in that hallway—where two young women saw me, and in seeing me, saw themselves differently.

That's the legacy—not just success, not just recognition, but **permission.**

THE INVITATION

So the question isn't whether you've learned how to code-switch.

Most of us have.

Instead, ask yourself:

- What would change if you stopped?
- Where are you still editing yourself?
- Where are you shrinking to fit expectations that were never designed with you in mind?
- Where are you holding back a voice that could shift the room—if you allowed it to be heard?

Because the truth is that you don't have to abandon awareness to be authentic. You don't have to reject professionalism to be whole. But you do have to decide that who you are is not something to manage.

It's something to lead with.

YOU WERE NEVER MEANT TO JUST FIT IN

I was given a name that opened doors. But I built a voice that changed what happened once I walked through them. And that's the work. Not just gaining access. But redefining what access looks like for those who come after you. Because you were never meant to spend your life adjusting to the room. **You were meant to walk in—and change it.**

ABOUT THE AUTHOR

B. MARIE ADAMS

B. Marie Adams is a two-time bestselling author, senior technology leader, and multi-venture entrepreneur who builds systems, spaces, and opportunities that empower underrepresented communities. With over 20 years of experience in IT leadership, she has led enterprise-scale initiatives impacting millions, driving innovation across government, banking, entertainment, and education sectors.

A recognized leader in DevSecOps, enterprise architecture, and software governance, B. Marie has received numerous awards, including executive and Presidential recognitions, and has contributed to cross-agency technology standards and transformation efforts. Her work bridges technical excellence with human-centered leadership, creating scalable solutions that improve systems and their people.

Beyond corporate, B. Marie is the founder of Entreherneur, a network supporting Black women entrepreneurs. With over 2,500 members, led to the creation of the Entreherneur Foundation, which provides funding and resources to Black women–owned businesses. She is also the creator of Brown Aspiration, a stationery and lifestyle brand that celebrates Black culture, identity, and ambition.

In 2021, she co-founded Pepperidge Promise LLC with her siblings, developing an agricultural and retreat space in Maryland focused on healing, sustainability, and community restoration. She is also the co-founder of Sapphire Rise, Inc., a STEM nonprofit expanding access to education and employment for underserved youth across Maryland.

A passionate mentor, speaker, and advocate, B. Marie is committed to developing the next generation of leaders—particularly women and minorities in technology, entrepreneurship, and STEM. She is a devoted mother and resides in Anne Arundel County, where she continues to lead with purpose, build with intention, and inspire others to turn access into impact.

AND JUST LIKE THAT

EXTENDING THE SHIFT

Presence, Vulnerability, and the Future of Authentic Leadership

"We are what we repeatedly do. Excellence, then, is not an act, but a habit."

—Will Durant

A NOTE FROM THE CURATOR

CHANTÉE L. CHRISTIAN

"Words mean more than what is set down on paper. It takes the human voice to infuse them with deeper meaning." —Maya Angelou

Somewhere along the way, life interrupted me in a way I could not plan for, prepare for, or push through. While bringing *Brave Spaces, Bold Conversations* to life, I found myself in the very work these pages invite you into. I had to create spaces, hold tensions, and tell the truth even when it would have been easier not to.

Everything in me wanted to keep going. I wanted to deliver, to honor timelines, expectations, and commitments, because that is who I have been.

And yet, I couldn't.

That reality humbled me in ways I am still learning how to articulate, because what I had to confront was not just the grief of one of my top five people on this planet, it was my identity. I find myself asking:

- *Who am I when I cannot perform at the level I expect of myself?*
- *Who am I when excellence looks like pausing instead of pushing?*
- *Who am I when I have to say, "I can't right now," not once, but more than once?*

That is a different kind of bold conversation. The kind we do not always have out loud. The kind that happens in the quiet, where there is no audience, no applause, and no outside validation.

Just you… and the truth.

The world is heavy, and people are carrying more than we can ever imagine emotionally, physically, and spiritually. Conscious leadership requires us to give rest to the tired ideology that says you must go with the flow or be the loudest in the room to make an impact. That is not where lasting change lives. Impact is found in the alignment between what you say, how you show up, and what you are no longer willing to ignore.

During the curation of this book, in an effort to convince my aunt to write a chapter, we discussed her career and the art of stopping people-pleasing and doing what was right for the collective. Unfortunately, a week later, she passed away, unexpectedly.

What she left me with was not a chapter, but a charge to continue to:

- move with excellence,
- understand that some people will only love you for what you can do for them,
- understand that not everyone is happy for you,
- decide regardless of the circumstances how you will honor your gifts and talents.

For me, legacy is not about performance. It is about the imprint you leave on the world. Those ripples. It is about refusing to bend so much that you break. That you lose yourself in the process of keeping the peace and not standing ten toes down on who you are and what you believe.

She taught me that being bold is not about being loud. It is about being clear. It is about standing in what you believe and letting your presence speak for you.

For those of you who have mastered the art of keeping the peace, hear me loud and clear. You get to teach people how to treat you and how to talk to you. En Vogue said it best, "Before you can read me, you got to learn how to see me."

I encourage you to see how you have been using your voice and see what your legacy will be. Using your voice is not just about what you say—it is about how you choose to be.

This book stretched me. AND it reminded me that this is not just a labor of love—it is an act of healing. I want to encourage and invite you to:

- Carry this forward.
- Embody what resonated.
- Release what no longer fits.
- Create and protect the kind of space you need.
- Create and protect the kind of space where truth is not just spoken, but lived.

What story will your ripples tell long after you're no longer in the room? Because your ripples are already telling a story. Is it the one you want them to tell?

ABOUT THE CURRATOR

CHANTÉE L. CHRISTIAN

Chantée L. Christian is an ambassador of awareness with two decades of experience in management consulting and coaching. As founder of My Best SHIFT, she helps leaders align strategy with self-awareness to lead with intention, clarity, and authenticity.

She brings a unique blend of emotional intelligence, business acumen, and social impact to clients across sectors, including Fortune 500 companies, nonprofits, universities, and federal agencies. At the core of her work is a commitment to being a catalyst for growth and change through inspired action.

Chantée is the founder of CC Media, the publishing imprint behind the acclaimed bestseller *Awareness Put Me On*. A 4x bestselling author and award-winning podcaster, she also created *Unspoken Truths of Being Black*, an award-winning series that explores critical issues through the lens of heightened awareness and lived experience. In 2021, she was recognized as a Northern Virginia 40 Under 40 honoree for her cross-sector leadership and community impact.

A lifelong learner, Chantée holds a bachelor's degree from George Mason University and an MBA from Webster University. She is a Professional Certified Coach (PCC), a Myers-Briggs Type Indicator (MBTI) Certified Practitioner, a Certified Change Management Professional (CCMP), and holds a Strategic Diversity, Equity, and Inclusion Management Executive Certificate from Georgetown University.

Beyond the titles and accolades, she's a true Aquarius who moves to the beat of her own drum. She enjoys a good libation, traveling, and shopping (even if only through the window). Most of all, she loves belly laughs and creating core memories.

ACKNOWLEDGMENTS

FROM CHANTÉE L. CHRISTIAN, WITH LOVE!

"It is curious that physical courage should be so common in the world and moral courage so rare." —Mark Twain

This journey has required me to do exactly what this book calls us to do: step up and step out of our comfort zones to create ripple effects far beyond our current sight. Bringing *Brave Spaces, Bold Conversations* to life has been a constant reminder that this work is not optional. It is necessary. This volume pushed me to remember why transparency, vulnerability, courage, and the willingness to be uncomfortable are essential if we want to make a lasting impact.

Somewhere along the way, I found myself using my voice even more than usual. Because we are living in a time where we must intentionally co-create brave spaces that invite conversations that are both bold and courageous. Change does not happen in silos. It happens when we come together and use our voices, which requires conversations.

As we worked on this project, I was reminded that this is exactly why I started *Unspoken Truths of Being Black*. It was a call to check in on my colleagues, create space for honest dialogue, and offer a platform where people could share their truths, offer insights, and move into inspired action.

What began as a conversation has continued to evolve into something much bigger. The Conscious Leadership Collective is a living example of what happens when people choose courage over comfort and use their voices to amplify one another. I am wildly excited and deeply proud of how far we have come in such a short time.

I wouldn't have survived this journey without the support, encouragement, and love of so many people, too many to name. If I didn't name you, please know that I love you and am forever grateful for your support and encouragement.

To my **parents**, thank you for allowing me the opportunity to use my voice. For encouraging me from a young age to dream bigger than what my eyes could see. Your egg is safe (if you know, you know). To **Samantha Armstrong**, thank you once again for being my right hand in this collection, so far. Your honesty and patience, and our never-ending GIF exchanges, have kept me grounded in more ways than I could share. I'm grateful for your friendship and willingness to keep showing up.

Talk about being in the right place at the right time. Thank you, **Jen Pihaja**, for inviting me into a space where I got to experience our amazing foreword author, **Reggie Hubbard**. Reggie, the way you tell a story and bring people along on a journey with you is top tier! In such a short time, you pushed me to be a better writer and storyteller. I appreciate you and your gift. It was serendipitous for us to meet when we did. And I will be forever grateful for your yes. Keep showing up as authentic and amazing as you are! The world needs you!

To our book cover designer, **Ida Brown**, thank you for being long with me on this ride. As we close the chapter on this *bright idea* of mine, I promise I won't have another one for at least a month or so (no promises). In all seriousness, I appreciate your willingness to push the envelope with me as we create lasting imprints on the world.

To the incredible **authors** of *Brave Spaces, Bold Conversations*, you all did the damn thing! I am so proud of you. I asked you all to go beyond the surface level and to lean into the moments where truth demanded to be spoken. And you did not disappoint. You brought your truth, courage, and lived experiences to these pages. In doing so, you gave others permission to see themselves throughout these pages.

Thank you for your courage, honesty, and willingness to step into this vision with me. I'm forever grateful for your "YES" to amplifying your voices and showing the world what conscious leadership looks like in real life.

Lastly, and certainly not least, to our family, friends, and supporters, **THANK YOU** for believing in us and supporting our dreams and being part of this journey with us. We hope this book meets you exactly where you are and encourages you to lean into the hard conversations with more courage and bravery.

REFERENCES

Introduction: *Brave Spaces, Bold Conversations* – Chantée L. Christian

1. Brené Brown, *Dare to Lead: Brave Work. Tough Conversations. Whole Hearts* (New York: Random House, 2018).
2. Naval Ravikant, quoted in Eric Jorgenson, *The Almanack of Naval Ravikant: A Guide to Wealth and Happiness* (Magrathea Publishing, 2020).
3. Neville Goddard, *The Power of Awareness* (New York: DeVorss & Company, 1952).

Chapter 1: *When Comfort Costs Everything* – Seema Patel

1. Brené Brown, *Rising Strong* (New York: Random House, 2015).
2. Alan Cohen, *A Deep Breath of Life: Daily Inspiration for Heart-Centered Living* (Carlsbad, CA: Hay House, 1996).

Chapter 5: *The Lion, the Bear, and the Giant* – Nayshondra Mercer

1. Dominique Hollis, "To Play or Not To Play the Game," *A Conscious Leadership Collective: Volume I: Leading From Within* (Arlington, VA: CC Media, LLC, 2025).
2. Luke 6:31, *Holy Bible*, New International Version.
3. 1 Samuel 17:33–37, *Holy Bible*, New International Version.
4. Matthew 18:15–17, *Holy Bible*, New International Version.
5. 1 Samuel 17:45, *Holy Bible*, New International Version.

Chapter 7: *My Leadership (And My Life) Rough Drafts* – Ernest Bonasera

1. Mel Robbins and Dr. Gabor Maté podcast conversation referenced in chapter discussion on trauma and leadership.

ABOUT

Brave Spaces, Bold Conversations is the second volume of the Conscious Leadership Collective, a thought-provoking anthology published by CC Media. Featuring a dynamic group of leaders, truth-tellers, and change agents across industries, this book explores the power of courageous dialogue, emotional fluency, and conscious choice in leadership.

Where Leading From Within invited leaders to begin with self-awareness, *Brave Spaces, Bold Conversations* explores what happens next—when awareness moves outward and leaders choose truth, candor, and accountability in the conversations that shape culture.

Far more than a collection of essays, *Brave Spaces, Bold Conversations* is part of a growing movement: amplifying honest dialogue, challenging silence and complacency, and using story as a catalyst for connection, accountability, and transformation. Each chapter is shaped through reflection, vulnerability, and collaboration to demonstrate what brave leadership looks like in action.

With nearly 60 authors supported through CC Media's publishing and coaching ecosystem, this work reflects our core values of authenticity, representation, courage, transformation, and truth. *Brave Spaces, Bold Conversations* isn't just a book—it's an invitation to create spaces where conversations that matter can finally happen.

THE SOUNDTRACK OF *BRAVE SPACES BOLD CONVERSATIONS*

Curated by the authors of *Brave Spaces, Bold Conversations*, this playlist continues the journey that began in *Leading From Within*. If the first volume held the rhythm of reflection and self-discovery, this one carries the sound of courage, candor, and truth spoken out loud. Every chapter, every song reflects the tension, honesty, and power that emerge when silence gives way to conversation.

SCAN TO LISTEN ON SPOTIFY

FEATURING SONGS LIKE: "BIGGER" • "BRAVE" • "LEGACY"

www.ingramcontent.com/pod-product-compliance
Lightning Source LLC
LaVergne TN
LVHW010607110826
845149LV00003B/799

* 9 7 9 8 9 9 9 5 4 3 3 9 4 *